Sensitivity: From a Burden to a Blessing:

How to be a Highly Sensitive Person to God's Glory

by
Launi Treece, PhD

ISBN: 1517226082
ISBN 13: 9781517226084
Library of Congress Control Number: **XXXXX (If applicable)**
LCCN Imprint Name: **City and State (If applicable)**

This book is dedicated to:

My husband—who has been my patient partner through this long process.

My children—the three treasures whom God saw fit for us to love and care for on this planet.

My patients—thank you for your trust and all you have taught me, which make me a better therapist all the time.

Rea Anne Scovill, Ph.D.—thank you for gently showing me I'm an HSP and leading me to be "a tree planted by water."

Highly sensitive Christians everywhere—God bless you!

Contents

Chapter One

God, Is There Really a Purpose to My Sensitivity?

A Description of the Highly Sensitive Person

Samuel[1] was referred to me by his medical doctor because I had provided psychological counseling to some of the physician's other chronic pain patients who also suffered from depression. When I first met Samuel, a tall forty-something man with soft brown eyes and graying hair, he did indeed appear very downcast. He had a presence about him that suggested he was one who had all of the strength and hope sucked out of him. He looked at me at times, but mostly he kept his eyes on the ground as he related the story of how he came to me for counseling. Just a few months before, Samuel had attempted to kill himself. He had been recovering from neck surgery due to an early injury, and the chronic, relentless pain was just too much to bear. He felt hopeless about pain relief. The surgery had not seemed to help at all, or perhaps it had even made his condition worse. He felt shame and regret for getting injured and then choosing surgery. He felt certain that he could not live life with this degree of incessant pain that he could not control. So he had gathered all the pain pills and sleeping pills that he could find, swallowed them with water, and lain down on the bed to die, clutching a photo of his family to his chest. When he was very near death, he felt a great sense of peace. But the next thing he knew, he

---

[1]. All patient names and details have been altered enough to protect patient privacy. Patients (happily) gave their permission for their stories to be told. Thank you!

was being revived in the hospital emergency room, feeling rather despondent that his plan had not worked.

As I got to know Samuel, I found him to be an extremely pensive, observant, and intuitive man. The pain he felt from his injury was intolerable, and the feelings of numbness and spaciness he felt as side effects from the pain medications were hardly any better. He visited many doctors, but they seemed baffled by the severity of his symptoms. He could observe and sense the doctors' ambivalence, irritation, confusion, and discomfort, which made the necessary doctor visits very hard for him to endure. Some doctors recommended antidepressant medications. Although he had tried these medications, the attempts would end in disaster because he would inevitably have a very difficult time with the side effects.

He was glad to come to our sessions. He would tell me that it was nice to have a doctor who would just listen and who seemed to understand him. I used common forms of treatment for his depression, including cognitive-behavioral therapy. This is a form of therapy that focuses on identifying thought and behavior patterns that have had a negative impact on the patient and purposefully determining healthier, positive, and rational thoughts and behaviors to pursue going forward. Although he took part in the therapy, his progress was slow. One day I explained to Samuel the concept of the *highly sensitive person*, originally coined by Elaine Aron, PhD.[2] I explained that Dr. Aron finds that approximately twenty percent of the world's population has a particularly sensitive nervous system. Samuel took the "Highly Sensitive Person" survey (see appendix A) and scored twenty-six points out of twenty-seven. This is an incredibly high score. I have never met a person who

---

[2]. I highly recommend reading Elaine Aron's book *The Highly Sensitive Person* (New York: Carol Publishing Group, 1996). In the book, the founder of the HSP trait gives an expert account of it. Please note, however, that Dr. Aron views spirituality mostly from a Buddhist approach, and not from a Christian one (see her "Comfort Zone" articles on spirituality in the May and August 2012 newsletters, found on her website called The Highly Sensitive Person at http://hsperson.com/comfort-zone/email-newsletters/).

scored twenty-seven and only a few who have even scored twenty-six. The knowledge and acceptance that he was a highly sensitive person (HSP) helped him start to make sense of everything that was happening in his life, including the intense sensitivity to his physical pain and emotional duress he was experiencing as a result of his disability. He intuitively knew the written format of Dr. Aron's book would be too overwhelming for him, so he bought the audiobook of *The Highly Sensitive Person*, knowing he would be able to process the input of the information more easily in an auditory format. He began to listen to the first chapter and found it to be excruciatingly accurate as a description of himself and his life experience. It was so painful and revelatory that he could only bear to listen to half of a chapter at a time, and sometimes he had to leave large periods of time in between his hearings so that he could process what he had heard within himself and with me in our sessions.

I am so pleased to say that today, after Samuel has taken the difficult but rewarding path of participating in therapy and self-awareness, he accepts and is learning to enjoy himself as a highly sensitive person. He has learned some coping strategies for his pain, and his suicidal thoughts have reduced from happening daily to being nonexistent. As his psychologist, I am extremely thankful that I was able to help him through those excruciating two years. I thank God for the privilege of being able to help my fellow brothers and sisters, and it is my prayer that I may be of help to all of you who are reading this book.

I am a follower of Christ. I am also a clinical psychologist. I have been in private practice since 1998 and have seen many changes in how we think of people, their minds, and how to help them cope, heal, and grow. In 2009, I learned about the concept of the HSP. I thought it was revolutionary and felt privileged to be one of the "few" who knew about this pivotal concept. Within a year's time, I had the honor of supervising two graduate students in psychology who were attending two different graduate schools. To my surprise, they were both being taught about the HSP in school!

The HSP concept has been entering into our culture's mainstream fairly rapidly.[3]

Often when I suggest to my patients that they may be highly sensitive persons, they react negatively, as if I have just been very critical of them. They are reacting to my statement as if I've said, "You're too sensitive," or "You are overreacting." In fact, the first time my therapist suggested to me that I was "highly sensitive," I felt the same indignant, misunderstood sting. She quickly explained to me the concept of the HSP and that what she said was not a critical statement about me but rather an indication of how finely tuned my nervous system is. I became interested. No one had ever told me about this concept before, and as my therapist described some of the traits of being HSP, I felt my mind recall memories of many HSP instances in my life when I acted as an HSP. The times when I had sensed that things were amiss yet other people were going on about their business as if all was normal. The times when I acted too mature for my age and, in sensing how others responded to me, behaved in a less mature way in order to fit in. So, I became intrigued and read Dr. Aron's book. In it, I found great reassurance for myself at forty-two years of age. I began to encourage my patients who seemed to have HSP qualities to take her survey. When I explained the concept to them, they typically felt a momentary sting and then a feeling of relief to know how they could better understand their experiences of this world. I have learned to be very careful of how I explain the idea of the HSP to my patients and make an effort for them not to feel ashamed or criticized but rather accepted and understood.

Dr. Aron believes that approximately fifteen to twenty percent of the world's population is HSP, meaning that a minor yet significant amount of people are highly sensitive.[4] She finds that it

---

[3]. See Andrea Bartz, "Sense and Sensitivity," *Psychology Today* 72, last modified July 22, 2014, https://www.psychologytoday.com/articles/201107/sense-and-sensitivity.

occurs equally in both men and women. However, it is not as socially acceptable for a man as it is for a woman, making it even more challenging to be male and highly sensitive.

Being an HSP is not a disorder or a diagnosis. It is simply the idea that just as some individuals are born with a sensitive gastric system, others are born with a nervous system that is more sensitive than the norm. This reasoning implies that it is a condition that would be genetically influenced. In fact, it appears that the HSP nervous system does run in families. In my own family, we see evidence that my mother, my oldest brother, myself, and two of my children all have highly sensitive nervous systems. We see how we are sensitive in different ways, or "flavors," as Dr. Aron describes. I am sensitive empathically; my mother, an artist, is sensitive to aesthetics; my son is sensitive to sound, visual input, and touch; and my daughter is sensitive to bodily sensations.

In looking at the Bible, one can see evidence of HSPs as well. One excellent example is that of King David, author of most of the Psalms. David was very observant of the majesty and beauty of God's creation, as he writes in Psalm 65: 9–13:

> You care for the land and water it;
> You enrich it abundantly.
> The streams of God are filled with water
> To provide the people with grain,
> For so you have ordained it.
> You drench its furrows
> And level its ridges;
> You soften it with showers and bless its crops.
> You crown the year with your bounty,
> And your carts overflow with Abundance.
> The grasslands of the desert overflow;
> The hills are clothed with gladness.
> The meadows are covered with flocks

---

4. Aron, *Highly Sensitive Person*, preface.

and the valleys are mantled with grain;
They shout for joy and sing.

King David also writes of his awareness of the sensations inside his own body, as in Psalm 22:14–15:

I am poured out like water,
And all my bones are out of joint.
My heart has turned to wax;
It has melted away within me.
My strength is dried up like a potsherd,
And my tongue sticks to the roof of my mouth;
You lay me in the dust of death.

There are many psalms that reveal how sensitive David was to the hidden, cruel intentions of others. Psalm 55:2–3 is one example:

Hide me from the conspiracy of the wicked,
From that noisy crowd of evildoers.
They sharpen their tongues like swords
And aim their words like deadly arrows.

When David was still a servant to King Saul, he was not only sensitive to his master's emotionally shifting states, he was also aware of how to calm and soothe him with music. King David was also very sensitive to spiritual stirrings. In Psalm 139: 7–10, he states:

Where can I go from your Spirit?
Where can I flee from your presence?
If I go up to the heavens, you are there,
If I make my bed in the depths, you are there.
If I rise on the wings of the dawn,

If I settle on the far side of the sea,
Even there your hand will guide me,
Your right hand will hold me fast.

King David was truly a man who was created to be highly sensitive and to write and sing from that awareness. We are blessed by his words and insights that have inspired generations.

What an HSP Is Not

Being an HSP does not mean that you are overly sensitive emotionally, such as being prone to taking things too personally or getting your feelings hurt, as people generally mean when they say in a pejorative way, "Oh don't be so *sensitive!*" It is certainly true that HSPs get their feelings hurt and can take things personally, so most have heard this statement many times. This causes great consternation for an HSP and builds up a defensive reaction of shame. They begin to feel like they *are* too emotionally fragile and that it is a very negative quality; one that gathers them negative attention that they feel all too acutely.

Christian HSPs can sometimes grow up thinking God made a mistake with them and that they just don't fit in with the rest of the world, or even in their own church. On the other hand, they can find great comfort in His word and in the gentle acceptance that Jesus shows to all kinds of people. Meanwhile, in the larger, harsh world where most people are not sensitive, life can be overwhelming for an HSP. King David needed to retreat to caves in the hills at the times when King Saul sent soldiers to execute him, and the psalms that seem to have been written during those cave moments (such as Psalms 55 and 143) suggest that he was overwhelmed with the harshness of this world and needed a respite so that he could only focus on God's care.

Likewise, HSPs often try to hide their sensitivities and can develop their own set of coping strategies, some of which are healthy and others that are unhealthy, as I will review in the following chapters. Sometimes my Christian patients wonder if God wove them inside the womb in such a way that they would have an ultrasensitive nervous system to ultimately serve His own good purpose. I cannot speak to God's ways, as we know that "His understanding no one can fathom" (Isaiah 40:28). I know that He made Adam and Eve perfectly and that that is how He intended for our world to remain. However, with the fall our world and our bodies have been tainted. I tend to think that variations in our bodily systems were not originally intended to cause us any hardship but rather to allow us to help one another as different parts of the Church body (1 Corinthians 12:14–31), encouraging us to enjoy and benefit from the blessings of the Christian community. I believe that being an HSP is a variation that perhaps has caused many people hardships in our tainted world but that God uses as a blessing for the HSP and those around him or her. You may be wondering if being an HSP is connected to the spiritual gifts, such as administration, encouragement, giving, hospitality, leadership, prophecy, teaching, or healing.[5] I have done some research on this and the findings are covered in my chapter five, where I look at community.

I suggest that being an HSP does not mean that one is automatically too emotional in reaction to stimuli. In addition, HSPs should not be mistaken for people who have a strong overreaction to stimuli based on past traumatic experiences. In my work as a clinical psychologist, I am trained to treat people with a wide variety of concerns. However, God has seen fit to draw me into the specialty of treating trauma survivors. I am very aware that individuals who have experienced trauma of any sort can have

---

[5]. See Bruce Bugbee, *Discover Your Spiritual Gifts the Network Way* (Grand Rapids, MI: Zondervan, 2005).

sensitivities to sudden changes in the environment (a heightened startle response or hypervigilance, for example) or to environmental cues that remind them consciously or unconsciously of the trauma. These cues, which we call "triggers," cause an anxious reaction in the survivor. For example, a person who has experienced the trauma of a gun fight may overreact to the trigger of hearing a car backfire. This kind of sensitivity is a physiological response specifically to the trauma and not in and of itself a sign of a person born with a sensitive nervous system. To be sure, HSPs tend to be more strongly affected by trauma when it occurs to them. However, overall, neither being emotionally fragile nor being sensitive to trauma triggers should be confused with being an HSP.

Nor is being an HSP the same thing as being shy or introverted. Certainly HSPs can also be shy and/or introverted, and perhaps they appear shy or introverted when they are retreating or holding back when their nervous system is on overload, but having these characteristics is different from being an HSP.

Author Sharon Heller, PhD, has written about sensitivities in a way that appears very resonant with the HSP concept. In her book *Too Loud, Too Bright, Too Fast, Too Tight*, she describes "sensory defensiveness" as a neurological condition in which one is easily overaroused by sensory stimuli. She states that evaluation and treatment by an occupational therapist is an excellent way to discern the extent and type of one's sensory defensiveness and that it should be treated with a "sensory diet." My son underwent occupational therapy from approximately age two to age six, and we are confident it greatly helped him to better self-regulate and cope with sensory input.

Just *How* Sensitive *Is* Sensitive?

Elaine Aron created the HSP self-test in 1996, and it is reprinted with the author's permission in appendix A. (For other tests such as the one to discern if your child is an HSP, please refer to her website: http://hsperson.com.) You may want to take a moment now to take the self-test. Your score will vary from zero to twenty-seven. A score of fourteen or more indicates you are a highly sensitive person. You will notice that the questions vary in what they are assessing. Some ask how you respond to loud sounds; others ask how you respond to intense emotional stimuli. Some are about noticing fine art; others are about being aware of how others feel and making a room of people more comfortable. Because the nervous system senses so many different aspects of this world, there are a myriad of ways that being an HSP can manifest for different people. For instance, one person may score a seventeen on the test and be particularly sensitive to sights, sounds, and tactile sensory input, while another who also scores a seventeen may be particularly sensitive to the moods and energy levels around them. For example, I tend to be high on the emotional-sensitivity and intuitive aspects of the scale, but my son is high on the nonemotional aspects of the scale. I can walk in a room and know what the mood of each individual is, but he would walk into the same room and notice how it smells and where the light is more intense. Once you have taken the test, reflect on the concept and notice your own sensitivities over time. Later you may want to take the test again to see if your score has changed due to your deeper understanding of what is being measured.

Although HSPs make up about twenty percent of the general population, they are estimated to be approximately eighty percent of most therapists' caseloads.[6] From my own experience, I would say this is true. Why would this be so? HSPs are more intuitive to their feelings and those of others and therefore are more inclined to seek therapy to sort out this awareness. If they experienced trauma, they are likely to have had a more intense reaction to it and

---

[6]. Elaine Aron, *Psychotherapy and the Highly Sensitive Person* (New York: Taylor and Francis Group, 2010).

therefore are seeking counseling to overcome their reaction to the trauma. They may feel misunderstood or even rejected by others for their worries and "overreactions" and want to seek the compassionate understanding care of a therapist. Some of my extremely sensitive HSP patients even came to counseling because they or their medical doctors feared they were going crazy! My HSP patients tend to have scores of twenty or above, and most of them range in age from thirty to fifty. These HSP patients are typically "burnt out" on the intensity that they see in the news, the negativity in their own communities, and the misunderstandings in their closest relationships. They are often inclined to help others and sense their needs quite well, but they have been met with irritation by those who do not see "what the fuss is all about." All of these are common and excellent reasons for HSPs to seek counseling.

One last comment regarding the scoring of the test: I imagine nervous system functioning as falling in a bell curve pattern, with the HSPs making up the higher end of the tail of the curve and another group of people making up the lower end of the tail. I call this latter group the "nonsensitives," and they may score a zero or one on the HSP test. As far as I know, there is no research on this concept to date. When I have suggested this idea to my HSP patients, they immediately respond that they have known nonsensitive individuals who have particularly caused them confusion, consternation, frustration, and even pain. All people tend to assume that other people in the world are similar to themselves. When HSPs come into intimate contact with nonsensitives, they are at risk of being shocked and even hurt! It can be helpful to explain to an HSP that this is a normal reaction for sensitive people when they are dealing with nonsensitive people and that the nonsensitive person was not trying to be difficult, it's just the way they are wired and they may not even know it! Sometimes, when I hear this type of complaint, I tell my patients of my own difficult experience with a nonsensitive person.

When I began my research for this book, I was eager to share my insights and discoveries with other Christians. I had done quite a bit of public speaking in the past, but being sensitive it had always been difficult for me to handle the challenges of public speaking. If there were one hundred people in the audience at a certain event, ninety-eight of them might have been smiling and nodding at what I was saying, but invariably I would only see the one who was falling asleep and the other one who was scowling at me. I decided to do the wise thing and take courses in public speaking so that I could learn to toughen up a bit and become a better speaker. So, I began trainings at a local Christian speakers' bureau and learned quite a lot from the primary teacher. Once I had a sample speech, I was invited to the teacher's home to give my speech to her, other vetted speakers in the bureau, and other students who were also giving speeches. If my public speaking skills were deemed worthy, I would be approved to join the speaker's bureau.

Of course, my speech was on the HSP concept. It was a small turnout that day, with only the teacher, one vetted speaker, and one other student. Before we gave our speeches, the teacher asked what degree of criticism we could handle as she gave feedback. Level ten indicated something like "As harsh as you wanna be, I can take it!" and level one was "I'm a weenie, please be uber-gentle!" This felt like a trick question to me. If I said a number too low, I would look fragile and weak, but if I said a number too high, I may get reamed! I decided to play it safe and say, "Five?" in a tentative voice.

When the teacher glanced at my speech title, she said, "Oh this should be good for me to hear—my teenager always tells me I'm too harsh and should be more sensitive." I gave my speech, making sure to make good eye contact, vary my intonations, and move slowly from one side of the podium to the other. At one point I had everyone in the audience take the HSP self-test. At the end of the speech, I sat back down, feeling pretty good about my performance. The teacher began by saying that she could not relate to my subject matter very well and that she had scored a one on the self-test. Immediately I could feel a flush of dread coming over me. Without skipping a beat, she launched into what felt like a tirade, explaining that I did not have what it took to be a public speaker. I began to silently cry and when the tears and snot became too messy I began to search the area for tissues. She did not read any of these cues and continued on to criticize me as a speaker, with examples of why she had come to her conclusion. I began to cry harder, sobbing audibly, with a shaky hand covering my eyes. I felt berated and ashamed, yet she continued.

I also felt the tension and indecision of the vetted speaker. She was sitting on the same couch as me, watching as her teacher, leader, and friend tore me apart and I broke down. As my sobs became heaves, she patted a hand on my leg and tried to interrupt the teacher to say a few positive comments on my speech. The teacher paid no attention to her cues and continued to degrade me, never asking me if I needed a break of some sort. At one point, I glanced over to the other student who had a far-off look on his face, as if he could not bear to be physically present in the room any longer. When the teacher was at last done with her chiding, she told me that she discerned I would likely never make a good public speaker but should instead write a book! Even though she may have been right, my patients, upon hearing this story, always assure me they think I'd make a great speaker (God bless them! I just hope I make a decent enough writer!).

So here was someone who knew she was perceived as insensitive, indicating that she thought she could modulate her interpersonal expressiveness by using a one-to-ten scale but who actually didn't have the ability or awareness to sense her own brusqueness or my extreme emotional reactions. If she *did* notice my crying, then she lacked any inner voice telling her to change her tack. My overall impression of her is that she is a kind-hearted, intelligent, and highly gifted speaker who truly loves the Lord. I believe she just was unable to think or react like a sensitive person in any given moment. For HSPs, this story is shocking. They would *never* be able to treat someone this way. They feel too conscientious to ever be hurtful to someone else, and because they feel the painful pang inflicted on the other person, tearing someone down would hurt *them* as well. But there are important places for nonsensitive people in God's kingdom as well! They have the type of Teflon coating that can allow them to be successful even in professions and ministries that are rife with criticism and attack (think of politicians, CEOs, and even head pastors).

Is This Book Useful to Me if I'm *Not* an HSP?

Absolutely! If HSPs make up roughly twenty percent of the population, then chances are you regularly interact with at least one HSP and the information in this book will greatly help you understand the person and get along more harmoniously with him or her. In my own case, my husband is not an HSP and we had been married for thirteen years before I discovered I was an HSP. I excitedly explained this to him. Once he could see how the description fit me, he had a noticeable look of "Ah-hah!" on his face. Finally he could understand that I was not being neurotic at certain times just sensitive. He had always admired that I was intelligent, but he could not understand how I would seem to take a small thing and turn it into a major concern. He would often tell me, "Just don't worry about it!" (in what felt like a harsh tone to me!). Now he could understand that I more acutely felt the negative aspects of this world and in addition that I was aware of subtle nuances that he was not aware of.

Together we reviewed a few of the ways he had not understood my concerns. In one instance, I had shared with him that I was particularly worried about a teenage girl in our congregation who often wore her disheveled hair as a messy veil over her downturned face. She almost never made eye contact with anyone and exuded a feeling of hopelessness. I asked him if I should share my impressions with the children's ministry leader. He thought I was reading too much into the situation. I prayed about it and felt the Holy Spirit confirm to me that I could carefully mention my concerns to the leader. When I told her my perceptions, the leader seemed surprised but assured me there were no home conflicts or other negative issues for this child as far as she knew. I continued to feel prompted by the Holy Spirit to pray for this girl. Within months, her father was removed from their home and a prayer request was put out to our church to pray for the family.

My husband could see in retrospect that my concerns were appropriate. Now he takes my concerns and observations as an asset to our family resources to help ourselves and others rather than a confusing irritation. Believe it or not, I am inclined to compare myself to a dog in terms of my role in the family. Let me explain. Dogs are born with a nervous system that can pick up on more sensory subtleties and extremes in our environment than a human, particularly in the area of scent and sound. We humans have used their abilities to assist in finding earthquake victims, sniffing out drugs or bombs, and serving as watchdogs.

Scientists have determined two opposing systems in the brain: the behavioral activation system (BAS) and the behavioral inhibition system (BIS). The BAS serves the purpose of sorting the information your brain gathers through the senses in order to discover data worth acting *toward*. The BIS serves the purpose of sorting the incoming data to discern what would be best to *avoid*. As an example, one of my fond memories from childhood is going wild mushroom hunting in the Pacific Northwest forests with my grandparents. One of the prized mushrooms we searched for was the tasty morel. What I recall is my grandparents showing me that the morels tend to grow near fallen logs and have whitish stems and spongy, tan tops. My BAS was really searching for the type of data my grandparents had shared with me, because it would lead me to the tasty prize I had eaten before when we took these mushrooms home and sautéed them in butter! However my grandparents also sternly warned me against picking any poisonous mushrooms. I'm sure they also gave me many examples of what these looked like, but all I recall is to "never eat red mushrooms!" My BIS system was keen to also look for red in order to avoid even touching these evil things!

One possible way to explain HSPs' nervous systems is that their BIS is operating more strongly than that of the average person.[7] This certainly hits home for most of my HSP patients. Although they can sense the positives around them, they tend to focus their mental energies on searching for the negatives around them that they seek to avoid. Alas, this tends to rob them of their joy. I often remind them to get back in touch with their abilities to sense positives around them. There is also a subset of HSPs that Dr. Aron calls "highly sensation seeking" (HSS). These people not only are sensitive to stimuli but *love* receiving it. They pursue sensory stimuli. I have an HSS patient who, once he finds a song he likes, plays it at maximum volume so he can feel it throughout his whole body. He can put the song on repeat and dance around the house basking in the words, beat, pitches, and volume. I tend to agree with Dr. Aron that his experience as an HSS is probably due to having a higher BAS than what is found in most HSPs and perhaps even than the typical person.

The notion of the higher level of BIS makes us return again to my "watchdog" concept. Am I the watchdog of the family? I guess that may be the case in some ways, but it can be a very good thing! It is very important that we learn to value those persons with a sensitive nervous system rather than dismissing them.

---

[7]. Elaine Aron, cited in Kathy A. Smolewska, Scott B. McCabe, and Erik Z. Woody, "A Psychometric Evaluation of the Highly Sensitive Person Scale: The Components of Sensory-Processing Sensitivity and Their Relation to the BIS/BAS and 'Big Five,'" *Personality and Individual Differences* 40 (2006), 1269–79.

I hope I have piqued your interest in the sensitive system. In the next chapter, we'll look at some examples from my own life and my patients' lives that will allow us to explore how although being an HSP can be challenging, you can turn it to your own, and more importantly, to God's advantage.

Chapter Two

God, It's So Hard Not to Worry!
HSP and the Experience of Anxiety

Anxiety is the clinical psychologist's way of saying "fear." Anxiety takes many shapes and forms, and can have a variety of diagnoses, but it all boils down to fear. Many of my Christian patients feel guilty that they feel fear because they know that Jesus himself directed us to "not be afraid" (see Luke 12:32 and John 14:27 for examples) and so it feels like a lack of trust and/or faith in our Lord if we succumb to fear.

So is fear all bad? God created us to experience the emotions that we have and I believe that each one, even the unpleasant ones, serve a purpose in our life. Fear is a useful emotion to alert us to a possible threat to our well-being. It is a part of the fight-or-flight autonomic nervous system response to potential danger. When our nervous system senses a threat in the environment, it alerts the mind and body, and the body in turn prepares to either run from or fight the danger. This response includes rapid, shallow breathing, a racing heart, and a feeling of fear or dread. This very feeling is often anxiety provoking in and of itself! At higher levels of intensity, this reaction is called a panic attack. One can see immediately why an HSP is more prone to anxiety than a non-HSP. HSPs have been soaking sensory input into their system to the point that they are already aroused at a higher-than-normal level. They are more prone to the "last drop in the bucket" nervous system spillover, which is a panic attack. In fact, when patients tells me that they have any history of panic attacks, I always screen them for being an HSP, and so far there has been a one hundred percent correlation!

HSPs' nervous systems are prone to anxiety for at least two reasons: First, this group notices signs of a potential threat more acutely than in those who are not highly sensitive. Most of the time these signs are not indicative of any serious threat, but still the HSP's nervous system notices them. For example, while driving on the freeway HSPs may be particularly aware of the pattern of cars around them, notice that cars are driving closer together and starting to hem them in, and then notice that they are beginning to feel anxious. Some HSPs become so regularly anxious while driving that they label driving as "too dangerous" and avoid it as much as possible. This is called generalization and can cause a person to limit his or her life. This is not what God calls us to do! He says, "I have come that they may have life, and have it to the full" (John 10:10).

Ways to Cope with Anxiety

As far as the HSP who has the sense of being hemmed in while driving, there are ways that they can use their sensitivities as an asset rather than a liability. Being hemmed in, in and of itself, is not a potential threat to the HSP driver. If it were combined with other factors, such as brake lights ahead or an erratic, swerving driver, then it might indicate a potential threat, but on its own, it is just a pattern of traffic. Moreover, being hemmed in is not a situation without options. HSP drivers can simply slow down until they find a way to move over to the slow lane and let that pattern of cars pass by. Being in the slow lane would also give them the option of easily leaving the freeway if they should feel overwhelmed. Just knowing they have options would increase their sense of control, which would reduce the anxiety.

In this example, one can see how the HSP originally used their senses to be aware of only the conditions leading to potential threat and then wanted desperately to exit the situation and avoid future ones. Another choice would be for HSPs to use the information about the situation to make choices to help themselves feel calmer (like moving to the slow lane), or to simply stay put in the conditions, knowing that remaining still will allow them to be attuned to any additional signs of true threat. While staying put, they can use their mind to visualize their driving options should the situation change. Being HSPs, they are going to be more quickly aware of their surroundings and of when the other cars are giving them opportunities for avenues of safe passage. This visualization is called mental rehearsal and it is a very healthy and empowering coping mechanism. We psychologists prefer that our patients choose to face down their fear in a situation like this one and cope with it in one of these ways, since facing one's fear is the fastest way to extinguish it.

Christians also have the power of prayer to extinguish fear. I strongly believe in the mighty power of prayer and that God attentively listens to each one. I also believe that some prayers can actually induce *more* upsetting emotions on the part of the person praying rather than leading them into a calmer mood. For instance, the HSP driver above may send up a prayer like this: "God help me! I'm overwhelmed here and so afraid. Please protect me from those other cars, keep them from hitting me and make them back off!" This is not a bad prayer, but notice how it keeps the HSP in a spirit of helpless victimization. It maintains the tone of the prayer and the focus upon the fear. Another way to pray might be "God help me, I know You are my strength. I feel overwhelmed driving here now. Please show me my options and give me wisdom on how to cope with this situation. Thank you for your help." You can see that this prayer focuses on God's resources, available to you, and leads you out of the fear of helplessness and into empowerment.

Many of my Christian patients have memorized scripture and they use that as a prayer in time of need. I refer my patients to the "My Scripture Cards" website (http://www.myscripturecards.com) for scripture cards to assist them with doing this. These sets of laminated cards have a theme printed on one side (such as "fear") and different scriptures on the other side to cope with that theme. They also have holes punched in one end and come with a key chain so you can easily keep them with you and flip through them until you find the one through which the Lord speaks to you in the moment. Elizabeth is a patient of mine who is relatively new to Christianity and does not yet know her Bible well, but she has already memorized Proverbs 3:5–6: "Trust in the Lord with all your heart and lean not on your own understanding; in all your ways acknowledge Him, and He will make your paths straight." Elizabeth is prone to panic attacks, but finds it a comfort that she can quote this awesome truth whenever she begins to feel fear. Perhaps the most powerful way to face fear is simply to say the name of "Jesus," invoking His presence and power. The Bible says there is power in His name (see Acts 3:16).

I had another HSP patient, Lucy, who was afraid to drive because she had a history of having panic attacks in her car while driving. Her fear of driving even led to the beginnings of agoraphobia, or the fear of leaving one's safe base, such as their home. When working with her I used my own format of systematic desensitization (a common technique to systematically break down what you fear into smaller chunks and learn to cope with the small chunks one at a time). Lucy would close her eyes and visualize the process of getting her two young children into the car, driving out of the neighborhood, over a floating bridge, and arriving at a mall. We would then play this over in her mind like a movie, stopping at the points in which her anxiety rose above a three on a scale of zero to ten. At those points she would explain why she was feeling anxious. It always had to do with sensory overload! From the very outset, before leaving the driveway, my patient noticed that she was having anxiety at the sound of her young child's chattering and/or the beeping or jangling sounds of her toys. She thought to give her child a toy to keep her preoccupied during the drive, but instead of reducing the noise, doing this created more noise than before!

Being a mother of three young children myself, I asked Lucy if her car had a built in video player, which it did. I had noticed that when I allowed my children to watch a movie in our minivan, they were amazingly quiet! I particularly liked to let them watch "Wally" since there is almost no dialog in that movie and many nice songs to listen to as I drive. I asked her if she thought having her kids watch a dvd movie would help them be quieter for the drive, and she said she thought it would. In fact, she even had a way for them to wear headphones while watching the movie, making her drive even quieter. We resumed the visualization "movie" of her drive to the mall, but this time imagining the children watching the dvd. She now rated her anxiety level as zero as she left the driveway, but later in the movie her anxiety would rise above three again. Each time she reported higher anxiety, we found solutions that she could picture doing to feel calmer. Eventually we created a visualization movie of her going to the mall in which her anxiety never went above a three. After that, we planned for her to drive to the mall on a Sunday morning, when traffic is at its lightest, using all the mentally rehearsed strategies. By this point, Lucy was already feeling more confident about driving with the children and was branching out on errands farther from home.

Anxiety that Feels Like an "Overwhelm"

The previous section describes the sensations of a panic attack and how to cope with them. However, for many HSPs the feelings of anxiety are more vague and free-floating, sort of like a cloud of anxiety that settles in around them, rather than the lightning bolt that is common of a panic attack. One reason this free-floating anxiety occurs for HSPs is because they have been soaking up stimuli, consciously or unconsciously, and feeling more aroused systematically in *every* way, not just negatively. Even joyful or neutral events can cause arousal. Researchers have found that the stress of losing a job can be equivalent to the eustress (positive stress) of getting married.[8]

One of my patients was referred to me by her psychiatrist because she was having some insomnia as well as fear of the *possibility* of insomnia. She took the HSP self-test and knew immediately that this described her. Over time we discerned that her sleep issues were caused by her sensations of overwhelm spilling into her time for winding down for sleep and into sleep itself. I taught her some techniques for better sleep, but what she said was even more helpful was when we focused on having her take some sensory breaks during her day to decrease that feeling of overwhelm. Throughout her day she would consciously choose to pause from her tasks and focus on rest and breathing. I taught her some deep-breathing techniques and showed her an app for her smart phone that guides people through breathing (there are many apps in this genre, but I like to show people Break Stress in Sixty Seconds by MyBrainSolutions).

She also liked a music CD by Dr. Jeffrey Thompson that I referred her to in which Dr. Thompson shares a music format he created. In these CDs different tones are played in your left ear than your right when you listen to it on headphones. As your brain synchs up the two hemispheres, Dr. Thompson claims it leads your brain waves into different patterns, such as ones associated with calm or even sleep. All of my patients have greatly benefitted from his soothing music that can be downloaded or played on a CD. Lastly, I had my patient focus on the present (a mindfulness technique). Doing this is calming because most anxiety is caused either by worrying about the past or about the future. When you stop and notice the present you are usually just fine! A useful

[8]. Holmes TH, Rahe RH (1967). "The Social Readjustment Rating Scale". *Journal of Psychosomatic Research* 11 (2): 213–218.

technique for focusing on the present is doing the "three-two-one" routine: notice three things that you currently see, hear, and touch; then, observe two of those three things; then focus on only one of the things. For example, "I see a lamp, the sky, and a pen. I hear birds, the clock, and the computer fan. I feel the floor, the pen and the chair." By the end of the exercise you say "I see a pen, I hear the clock, and I feel the floor". It's an easy method to use in almost any situation. She told me that when she used one or more of these techniques several times during her day, her sleep time went much more smoothly and her overall fears of sleep improved.

Grant, another patient of mine, would become overwhelmed at parties. He described a time when he accompanied his girlfriend to a party at the home of one of her friends. He was almost immediately overwhelmed by the sensory input of multiple voices, music, and interpersonal dynamics and by his own reactions to them, intake of new smells and sights, and the unspoken pressures of needing to be liked. His girlfriend found friends to chat with. He noticed a fish tank in the corner of the living room and found a place to sit near it, where he could rest his eyes on the soothing sights of the floating fish and the sounds of the consistent bubbles. Now, as people would come by to talk with him, he could handle the interchange well because he had found a way to buffer and limit the sensory input of his environment. Grant left the party feeling confident of how he handled it and more prepared for future parties he may be "dragged" to.

Another patient of mine, Stuart, is sensitive to many things in his surroundings, but is particularly sensitive to the passage of time. He can literally *feel* the passing of a minute, even while engaged in very high-level cognitive functions for his job. He, like most HSPs, is very conscientious and concerned with not being late. He feels irritation when others are late or if it appears that they will be late, and he experiences great distress if he himself will be late or keep others waiting due to circumstances beyond his control. Stuart has learned to be assertive about maintaining his boundaries related to time. He arranges his work and personal schedule so that there are gaps of open time in which he can catch up and not fall behind in expectations of him. Of course he gives himself more than enough time to arrive at any appointments and he is *never* late to my appointments! Since he often arrives forty-five minutes ahead of his scheduled time, he usually finds a quiet place to park near my office and read. He has found ways to adapt to his own flavor of HSP and not become overwhelmed in his day.

Yet another patient of mine has noticed that when she becomes overwhelmed in her nervous system, she has a need to "cocoon." She (and several of my other patients as well) has a special chair that she can settle into, with sides or pillows that help her feel gentle pressure and the feeling of being surrounded, or covered. Sometimes she finds a way to feel surrounded by wearing a backpack or fanny pack when she is out in the real world. When she goes to functions, like a wedding, she carries a sweater, vest, or coat (depending on the weather) to lie across her lap. For her, the key is being prepared to have these tools at her disposal and using cocooning/covering throughout her day to rebalance her nervous system.

As for myself, I can very much relate to the feeling of overwhelm in my daily life. I thank God for guiding me to being a psychologist because it is about the best job for an HSP! I can (typically) focus on one person at a time, I get to use my empathy skills to be helpful to others, and I can control my office and my schedule. However, I spend twenty-seven hours seeing clients a week, which is considered full time for a psychologist considering the extra hours of writing notes, letters, disability paperwork, returning and making calls, handling the billing, cleaning, and so forth.

When I'm not at work I am a very active mother of three children. In the past, I described to my therapist that I sometimes felt guilty about how I interacted with my children because when I reached a point of overwhelm I would sort of "growl" at them.

Often, after a long day of work, I'd get down on all fours on the carpet and all three kids would join in on pretend play of climbing and wrestling with me. There would be tickling and, of course, the children would squeal and holler with delight. I enjoyed all this hub-bub, too, picking up on the delicious energy of their delight, but inevitably I would become the mamma lioness who can no longer tolerate the cubs climbing on her, swatting at her tail, and biting her ear. I would then roar, "Enough!" and stand up suddenly with a child usually thumping to his or her feet in surprise. I would go from feeling excited and joyful to feeling irritated and overwhelmed, which then led to guilt at ruining the party. Now, I still wrestle with the kids and let them know when I've reached my limit, but I no longer feel guilt at winding down the party (more slowly now). I know I am an HSP and it is okay to have boundaries. I can feel good about modeling for my children that there is a time and place for all emotions and activities and it is natural to transition out of a situation when you feel the need to. As written in Ecclesiastes 3:1: "There is a time for everything, and a season for every activity under heaven."

Worrying

Worrying is a milder version of fear. There is a clinical term for it called "rumination," but I like to describe it to my patients as "marinating" in your worrisome thoughts. The same fears keep circling round and round in one's mind and it can become quite draining. HSPs are more prone to worrying as a result of picking up on subtle signs and trying to understand what they mean or indicate. For instance, an HSP may pick up on the subtle nonverbal cues in another person, such as their facial expression, eye contact, body language, or tone of voice, and from there marinate in what they think the other person is thinking or feeling. Typically, the HSP then takes it one step further and assumes the person was specifically thinking or reacting to them. "Did that gruff tone of voice mean that person was angry at me?" "Did the lack of eye contact mean I disappointed my friend?" We humans are so prone to selfishness and pride, and Satan has known and exploited this weakness from the very beginning. He meets us in these worries and creates unnecessary fear by casting his lies. He might say, "Yes, I'm quite sure you disappointed your friend, because you really aren't that great of a friend anyways. Think of all the things you've done wrong. You may not even be able to fix this friendship. He's probably given up on you already." Part of the work I do with patients (a variation of cognitive therapy) is to identify the lies and replace them with the truths. I let them know that the truth of the situation is not as bad as their marinatings have made it out to be, if they examine the evidence. The truth is that "God gave us a spirit not of fear but of power and love and self-control" (2 Timothy 1:7).

Some HSPs experience worries because they know they are sensing more than others do, and this causes them to feel a degree of responsibility that rises above that of the average person. They feel obligated to take extra measures to create safety and peace in their surrounding as much as possible. Sometimes this is possible, but all too often the circumstances are not within their control. This can cause responsibility-prone HSPs to feel anxious that they *should* intervene, even if they know they cannot for practical reasons. At one time, I became concerned for a non-HSP patient because her husband sounded like he was being overly controlling and overbearing. He seemed to be demanding and micromanaging my patient from how she described his actions. Since I did not know her husband very well, I arranged for a release of information to be signed by him so that I could speak with his individual therapist. His therapist knew him well and assured me his actions were not those of control but of protection, which I was very relieved to hear. She said that her patient is an extremely sensitive person (I would not be surprised if he ranked a twenty-six or higher on the test) who also went through abuse as a child. He adores his wife and children and would do anything in his power to protect them. As he became aware of any potential threats, he would sometimes come across as being strident in his requests. Once I explained the HSP concept to his wife, his actions made complete sense to her and she no longer viewed him as controlling but rather as loving. They developed better ways to talk through the tense times when his alarm bells were a bit too dissonant to her ears!

Again, some HSPs feel overly distressed and responsible when things turn out for the worse in a situation, feeling guilty about not being able to change the circumstances and watching as others make mistakes. Elizabeth feels a pang of embarrassment or shame on the behalf of others when she perceives they've made a bobble of some sort. She realizes that they may have just let it go and gone on about their day, or never even realized it in the first place, but she finds it hard to let go of *their* shame. I couldn't resist asking her if she had ever felt that way with me, and she shyly answered, "Yyyesssss..." It was in regard to a time when she desperately needed to set up an intake appointment with a psychiatrist, but I had no psychiatrists to refer her to that would get her in to see them immediately. From Elizabeth's perspective, this was something I should have been embarrassed about, so she fretted about it *for* me. I explained to her that I of course *did* know some psychiatrists well and referred patients to them, but it would be unethical for them to move someone to the head of the list because *I* requested it. Once she better understood the sad dearth of psychiatrists in our area and the ethical guidelines, she was able to let go of those worries on *my* behalf! I am grateful that we have a good-enough rapport so that we could work through those feelings, but so often in life we do not have the opportunity to just go back to the person and "get it straight," so to speak. Elizabeth is learning to shed off others' missteps and return again to focusing on herself.

HSPs are human and must be careful not to err in pride, placing themselves in the position of God. God sees everything that other person did (and thought!), and it lies between that person and God. The serenity prayer can be so helpful in these circumstances, allowing us to recall that we can even have serenity over the things we cannot control because God is in control! For those who do not have the serenity prayer memorized, it flows as follows: "God grant me the serenity to accept the things I cannot change, the courage to change the things I can, and the wisdom to know the difference."

Addiction?

One might intuitively guess that the HSP is more prone to develop addictions than a non-HSP. One might assume that HSPs would turn to alcohol, drugs, or medications to reduce the intensity of their awareness. From my experience in my private practice, I hear from my HSP patients again and again that they tried alcohol or drugs as a teenager. Sometimes out of curiosity; sometimes out of a need to fit in; sometimes to self-medicate their feelings of overwhelm. However, when they consumed alcohol or drugs, they acutely noticed the numbing or stimulating effect on their mind. This lack of complete control caused them intense anxiety and they wanted nothing more to do with mind-altering substances. In fact, this effect often poses a problem for HSPs with their prescription medications. If there is an effect or side effect, they will notice it and not be able to ignore it. I write more on this subject in chapter four. I am sure there are exceptions to this rule and there are HSPs who have addictions to substances, but I would hazard a guess that the addiction rate is much lower among HSPs than it is among non-HSPs.

Chapter Three
God, Why the Burden on My Heart?
HSP and the Experience of Depression

Just as there are many forms of anxiety, there are many different ways to experience depression. Depression is a subjective feeling of sadness, helplessness, hopelessness, and/or worthlessness. If often is accompanied by decreased energy, decreased enjoyment in life, and changes in appetite or sleep. Sometimes the depressed person feels more irritable as well. Although the primary mental health concern for an HSP is anxiety, there are reasons why HSPs can be prone to depression as well.

Low Self-Esteem

As mentioned earlier, an HSP will notice any indication that their words or behaviors are disapproved of. If they grew up in a home or church environment where shame or criticism were used to shape the child's behavior, they may have been given a negative self-image telling them that they were inadequate. Any child may develop that self-image, however, an HSP child is particularly sensitive to even subtle indications of falling short. This self-image carries into adulthood as a learned approach and response to their environment. One can imagine how this leads to a chronic feeling of worthlessness or depression.

Remember Samuel in chapter 1, the patient I helped to get over his suicidal feelings? He had the misfortune of being primarily raised by a harsh and critical mother. His father, although being a kind person, had a severe heart condition and was weak in energy, and the family was instructed to let him rest calmly. Samuel was a bright and talented young boy. Sometimes his teachers would compliment him for his artistic and singing abilities. His heart would rise up with the hope being complimented brought him about his innate abilities in the arts and the enjoyment he felt. However, if he told his mother of a compliment or if the teacher mentioned it to his mother, she would find a way to cut him down and discredit the compliment. She seemed to feel disdain for his achievements, as if he would become smug if he took pride in them.

Let us take a moment to acknowledge that all abilities and gifts we have are gifts from God; we would be amiss to take self-centered pride in them. However, because Samuel was not taught how to enjoy and expand upon his God-given gifts in a way that "boasts in the Lord" (Jeremiah 9:24), he became hopeless about enjoying his gifts and learned ways to "disappear" and blend into his environment so that he would not be noticed in positive *or* negative ways. As a young man, he chose to enter the military. He knew he was a sensitive man but also knew that being sensitive was a trait that was devalued or even denigrated in men. He chose to work in the military to hide his emotional style and fit in with fellow men as a tough soldier. Later in life, he continued to try to pursue "macho" jobs. He became a contractor, since it allowed him to show his physical strength and defy danger every day on his job. He secretly still enjoyed his aesthetic touch. He shyly told me in one session that as he would drive away from a finished job, he would look in the rearview mirror to admire how good the remodel job looked and how pleasing it was to the eye.

As he continued to act the part of the macho man, people began to expect this persona from him. He became more dissatisfied and depressed at the feeling that he was being disingenuous. He eventually became more introverted, shying away from social interactions. One day he hurt his neck on a job, leading to the relentless pain I described in chapter one. As he could no longer work, part of his emotional therapy was to return to one of his original loves: singing. He is now enjoying singing karaoke at home with family or even in bars.

I once mused out loud to him in one of our sessions that I wondered if HSP children who were raised by mean parents were inclined to either be particularly kind when they became parents or to decline to have children altogether. I wondered if they felt the harshness of their parenting so acutely that it would make an impression on them and they would only choose to be a parent if they could be certain that they would never repeat the pattern. He was silent, and I must have suggested that he could think about my statement and we could talk about it later if he wished. A few days after that session, Samuel sent me an e-mail, which he gave me permission to quote:

> You're right. I do process things we talk about in our sessions on the way home and even for a few days after. The discussion about HSPs in the last moments was particular food for thought...I believe if HSPs are given the tools to understand their inherent abilities early on, they can become successful in even the most strenuous of occupations if they think what they are doing is for the greater good and it's morally just. I think true HSPs are born with a mental compass (no matter what forces may try and obscure that compass) that steers them toward what is right and good. I think it is harder to corrupt an HSP than someone who is not one. I think HSPs would rather diminish their own lives than diminish the lives of others unless it was somehow justified by their compass. I would imagine war or combating evil would be a couple rare instances where the inherent self-sacrifice born into HSPs would be set aside for

the achievement of the greater good. I think HSPs that are stunted, for whatever reason, from understanding what sets them apart from the vast majority of people (abuse being one form of scrambling their signals) still possess their compass and would rather live in obscurity than to lash out and hurt innocence in retribution for the way they were treated. I think abused HSPs will most likely lead an extremely difficult, ungratifying life for much of their life. Unable to lash out and relieve their pain by hurting others for the pain they suffered, they are relegated to travel a lonely road, exercising great patience, hoping and praying that someday the mystery in them would be revealed. They are even resolute in the fact that it may never be revealed, but it is of no consequence as long as they leave no unjustified destructive mark on another's soul. All this is to corroborate your preliminary assertion that abused HSPs probably don't perpetuate the abuse cycle as much as non-HSPs. See ya next time.

As you can see, being an HSP and emotionally abused as a child led Samuel to an often-lonely and depressing life. He keenly and painfully knew he had special gifts but could not feel comfortable in the way he naturally expressed them. So, he pursued careers in which he covered up his sensitive tendencies but felt was being disingenuous in how he was being in the world. This reminds me of another patient, Anna, who knew from a young age that she was particularly intelligent. She did well in school, which was pleasing to her and to her parents. But soon she felt the pressures of her parents to achieve, mostly in order to satisfy their own desires to leave a legacy and make them "look good." Torn now, she began to falter in her academic efforts. This caused her parents and teachers to be disappointed. She knew she had great potential, yet she was underperforming. The shame she felt for this was paralyzing, causing a downward spiral. She did go on to college and eventually went into a specialized career in helping disabled children, which would be most gratifying. However, her sensitivities to her own disingenuous efforts also caused her grief and sadness for much of her earlier life as well.

Helplessness

As stated in the chapter on anxiety, HSPs are typically very conscientious. They can quickly assess what is needed to make a room feel cozier or to help resolve a tense situation. They are typically excellent at giving advice and guidance to those whom they know. One of my HSP patients, Joe, cannot help but witness the needs, spoken and unspoken, of those around him. He feels compelled out of a kind heart to offer suggestions and help. Sometimes this is met with gratitude, but at other times the individual interprets Joe's help to be intrusive, unnecessary, or controlling. Often the individual does not follow his suggestions and Joe feels helpless and rejected as he watches their negative circumstances worsen. I imagine he can relate to the young boy in the movie *The Sixth Sense* who says, "I see dead people...and they don't know it!" This experience is very depressing for him. In addition, he is very attuned to both people's spoken words and their nonverbal communication. He becomes very perturbed when these do not line up, which he often perceives as lying, yet he finds it hard to confront the people for fear that they are either not aware of their true feelings or motives or do not want them exposed. Again, this experience causes him great frustration and helplessness, leading to a stuck feeling of depression.

Sometimes, the other person is delighted by Joe's help and begins to use him in response. At first this is of no consequence to him as the joy of helping others outweighs the pain of being used.

However if it continues for too long, he begins to feel resentment (and guilty for that feeling!), which can also lead him into feeling depressed and isolated from others.

For Joe, the awareness that he is an HSP and how this leads to his desire to help others are helpful. It allows him to be aware that this is just how he is and he cannot change his heart from warm and caring to aloof. He is working on looking for the subtle signs of those individuals who are both open to his help and not likely to abuse it, whom he will start focusing his attention on. We are currently working on focusing some of his attention on himself and his own needs, too!

Depression Resulting from Trauma and Abuse

The Lord has led me in my career path to the treating of trauma. It is deeply gratifying to me to assist (with the Lord's direction and power) in the healing of my patients' deep wounds from trauma. Many of these wounds go back to broken childhoods. In 1998, I was trained in the treatment method called Eye-Movement Desensitization and Reprocessing (EMDR). This is a method where the patient recalls the traumatic event while being given bilateral stimulation through left-to-right eye movements, vibrating handheld pads, and/or music/tones on headphones.[9] By using bilateral stimulation while the person is recalling the event, both the left (verbal/analytical) and right (emotional/spatial) hemispheres are being activated and processing the information (in regular talk therapy, it is possible for mainly the left hemisphere to be activated, but not so much the right). I have seen this technique work in amazing ways over and over again. Where patients were once stuck in the pain, they found freedom from the memories and

---

[9]. This technique was first discovered by Francine Shapiro. For more information, I recommend you peruse the EMDR International Association website at http://www.emdria.org.

a renewed, wider perspective, which was healing and encouraging. I liken it to monocular versus binocular vision. When you see something with *both* your right and left eyes, you have better depth perception, allowing you to put your experiences in perspective. With EMDR, you realize that you have survived, that there is actually space between yourself and the trauma.

Originally rising out of EMDR work, Peggy Pace created another in-depth form of treating trauma called Lifespan Integration (LI).[10] I describe LI as extremely healing and elegant inner-child visualization work. In this therapy, people recall the event from the perspective of the age they were when it occurred. For instance, they may recall being eight years old and watching their parents verbally and physically fighting. Then they picture their present-age self stepping into the scene and helping the younger self change or cope with the situation for the better. For Christians, it can be especially helpful to have Jesus enter the scene, too. The adult self will ask the younger one, "What would you like me or Jesus to do to make this better?" If the child replies that he or she wants Jesus or the adult self to make the parents stop fighting, then that is what happens. This continues until the child feels better. Then the adult (and Jesus) takes the child to a safe and peaceful place to review images of growing up to his or her present age. These events in one's life are organized as memory "cues," which the patient writes down and brings to the session and then gives to me to read to them. I ask that the cues be neutral to positive. This section is extremely healing for the patient as they see that they really did survive the trauma and some good things follow in life. It ends by bringing the younger self to the present-day and showing them they are safe and loved now.

At one time, I worked with Phil, a quiet-spoken and gentle man in his forties. His wife encouraged him to see me since she was

---

[10]. For more information, please go to the Lifespan Integration website at http://lifespanintegration.com.

concerned that their almost nonexistent sex life was due to his history of sexual abuse by a family member. His wife was very sad to see how deeply he was still negatively impacted by his abuse. As I do with most all of my trauma patients, I explained that both EMDR and LI are excellent options to use to assist the healing process. Often the patient will try one and then the other to see which one they prefer. With Phil, both methods worked, but he preferred LI. As with most of my patients, he felt a great sense of peace and purpose when he reviewed his life in total, both the good and the bad. His abuse would be horrific for any person to endure, but he was particularly tortured by holding it inside all these years in order to protect others from either hearing the ugly facts or believing the atrocious actions of a family member. Phil's sensitivities would have made it a double reliving of his pain to explain it to others, in that he would feel both his own pain and other's shock and pain upon hearing it. He felt more at ease describing the trauma to me, a trained professional, in an environment where he could close his eyes while telling the story and not have to be aware or track my reactions to his story. He often thanked me for the intense relief he had during lifespan integration at finally being able to express what happened to his very sensitive and loving young self.

Toward the end of our work together, at the end of a particularly difficult session, I asked Phil if he would be okay for the rest of the day. He said he would be okay because he would give himself time in the garden. Curious, I asked him what his garden was like. With a shy smile and a sparkle in his eye, he humbly explained that he was particularly sensitive to enjoying scents. He had researched and noticed different plants and trees that have strong and pleasant odors. He had created his own private garden filled with these plants, and on the days he needed refreshing he would meander in his garden, sometimes plucking a leaf or pulling the pine needles and breathing in the sweet pungent smells. I told him I was incredulous at the creative and wonderful way he had honored his sensitivities and need for regrounding and healing by creating this special place for himself. I think we all could take a lesson from Phil to use our sensitivities to our benefit by creating our own special sensory retreats.

One more point to make about trauma and the HSP: A natural and unconscious coping mechanism people of all ages do when under severe trauma is to dissociate. Dissociation describes the experience of the mind disconnecting from the body in order to blunt the full experience of the traumatic event. If an HSP has used dissociation through much of his or her life as a coping mechanism, the person can eventually feel an overall blunted reaction to the world. When that individual first takes the HSP self-test, the score may be falsely low. From my experience, I had to sit with these individuals over time to see their "true HSP colors" come out and explain to them that they are HSP at the core, yet have been going through life in a somewhat dissociated fog. Often these patients are relieved and grateful to acknowledge, respect, and return again to their true sensitive selves. They find great solace in their turnings to God, Jesus, and the Holy Spirit, whom they can sense again and whose comfort, peace, and direction assist them in their discovery and healing of their earlier wounds. Their experience reminds me of Psalm 23, which so beautifully reminds us of His loving, gentle care:

> Even though I walk
> through the valley of the shadow of death,
> I will fear no evil,
> for you are with me;
> your rod and your staff,
> they comfort me.

Chapter Four

God, I Think My Body is Saying Something. Am I Crazy?
The HSP and Medical Concerns

Injuries and illnesses can be particularly upsetting for HSPs. Many an HSP has been referred to my office when they have undergone all appropriate and helpful medical interventions, medications and physical therapies, yet still experience life altering pain, discomfort or disability. These HSPs describe, often poetically, their internal bodily sensations. I have heard joints described as "zippers" or "gears" grinding, bumping or overlapping in odd ways. HSPs sometimes sense their body to be making sounds inside, like a squeaky door or heavy clunking. As you can imagine, these sensations are quite distracting and troubling to an HSP who has become totally attuned to how their body is supposed to feel and sound.

To make matters worse, sometimes doctors do not relate to these subjective descriptions. They look for hard evidence in MRIs and x-rays but the injury or problem may be too subtle to be seen by objective measures. I have great admiration for medical professionals. They must be incredibly intelligent to enter medical school, and then they must successfully endure their internship and residency. Dr. Aron supposes that due to the high degree of stress, stimulation, sleep deprivation, and intense emotional aspects of medical school and training, very few HSPs can successfully complete the program, thereby implying that very few medical doctors are HSPs. I have asked my medical doctor friends what they thought of this concept and they wholeheartedly agreed!

My HSP patients describe to me again and again that they can exquisitely sense when something is amiss internally. They feel bodily sensations that non-HSPs would either barely notice or be able to ignore or distract themselves from. HSPs, however, cannot easily ignore the bodily symptoms so they take it to their doctors. The doctors are usually overworked and extremely busy and are interested in seeing patients who are in immediate distress receive medical help as quickly and efficiently as possible. When an HSP comes to the doctor's office complaining of a symptom that the physician either cannot see objective evidence of or cannot see evidence of there being any serious problem, the doctor may unwittingly show signs of reproach or dismissiveness. The physician often has other patients who are in clear distress and need of care and sometimes refers the HSP patient to a psychologist or psychiatrist to determine if he or she needs mental health care for anxiety or may be a hypochondriac who is merely seeking attention. When I explain to these patients that they are not "crazy," that I believe that they are truly noticing something amiss in their bodies, and that they are simply born with a sensitive nervous system, they are greatly relieved. With my HSP patients, we work on assertiveness and communication skills, rehearsing how to talk with medical providers to explain bodily experiences and request help.

For one of my patients, one of her greatest inspirations to keep trying was the thought of what Christ endured on the cross. His painful sacrifice gave her motivation to push through her own painful experience and to keep striving for a better life. Christ is familiar with all of our pain, having endured it while He was here on Earth, which should give us great comfort. As stated in Hebrews 4:15–16:

> For we do not have a high priest who is unable to sympathize with our weaknesses, but we have one who has been tempted in every way, just as we are—yet without sin. Let us then approach the throne of grace with confidence, so that we may receive mercy and find grace to help us in our time of need.

Jake was referred to me through medical channels. Jake had recently undergone severe medical symptoms, most likely associated with high-intake, chronic alcohol abuse. When he admitted to his medical doctors that he did use alcohol almost daily, they became concerned and sent him to therapy to work on his "alcoholism" issues. Jake was scared. The bodily symptoms he had recently endured and the drama of the hospital stay and interventions had taken a huge toll on him. He was committed to examining his alcohol use and do what it took to control it. When I conducted an interview to determine the extent of his alcohol use, I was stymied. His use was above average, but not much above. It certainly didn't warrant the medical issues he was having. In graduate school, we were taught to always assume patients will underreport their alcohol and drug use, so I warily looked at him and sternly warned him he would only get better if he is totally honest with me. He immediately had a stunned look on his face and promised me that he was being honest. On that awkward note, our session ended. He came early to our next session and we went through some more awkwardness while we talked about my concerns regarding his actual alcohol use and his own sincere attempts to be totally honest. I sensed I could trust what he had said about his alcohol use not being severe. We both agreed, however, that it would be best for him to go alcohol-free for the time being in the hopes that his body would heal more quickly and fully.

Over time, it became apparent that Jake was an HSP and was incredibly aware of the subtle nuances in his body sensations at any given moment. If he did not have a clear explanation for a physical feeling, then he was prone to worry about it. Sometimes he would even worry about worrying! After all, too much cortisone and adrenaline is not good for the body, right? We shifted our focus from his alcohol use to his learning to honor his body and what it was telling him without overreacting to it. Eventually his medical doctors found that his original issues were not related to alcohol use but rather to a more rare cause. This vindicated him and he did try to drink a few beers after that. However, he found that alcohol no longer was tempting to him. He had learned, in the meantime, other ways to cope with his stressful, busy days and found that clearheaded play with his young children was more therapeutic than a drink.

Medically Sensitive

Michael Jawer is a leading specialist in studying some of the more confounding medical symptoms, such as sick building syndrome, environment toxicity, and chronic fatigue syndrome. In his opinion, there is a subset of humans who are more sensitive to environmental toxins or unhealthy components. He thinks of these people as sort of humanity's "Canary in the coal mine." He is aware of the HSP concept and is open to the idea that the highly sensitive individual would, at the very least, overlap with the physiologically sensitive individual.[11]

In my own caseload, I have witnessed an HSP patient go through the turmoil of multiple Western medical interventions as well as naturopathic interventions, trying to understand her unique set of symptoms. Over time it became clear she had chronic fatigue syndrome as well as multiple nutritional allergies. Most of her help came through naturopathic avenues, being very diligent with what she ingested, and trying to regularly exercise. Mercifully, while she

---

[11]. Michael Jawer and his coauthor Marc Micozzi, MD, PhD, have written an excellent chapter in *The Spiritual Anatomy of Emotion* (Rochester, VT: Park Street Press, 2009), pp 244-255 in which they outline different ways to explain human sensitivity. Some of the ways they mention are inborn sensory differences, HSP, sensory defensiveness, sensory processing disorder, thin boundaries, somatization, overexcitabilities, absorption, fantasy proneness, and transliminality.

was exploring how fragile her body was to her physical world, she was also drawing closer to God. She was deeply spiritual, almost mystical. She found intense healing and hope through intercessory prayer. She deeply connected with teachings at the School of Healing Prayer (See http://www.christianhealingmin.org) and also delved into prayers to heal generational sins in her family. In our sessions, Lifespan Integration proved very healing for her. Although it forced her to come face to face with her own fragility, it also allowed her to be certain of God's strength, mercy, and power to heal. This reminds us of Paul's testimony in 2 Corinthians 12:7–9:

> Therefore, in order to keep me from becoming conceited, I was given a thorn in my flesh, a messenger of Satan, to torment me. Three times I pleaded with the Lord to take it away from me. But He said to me, "my grace is sufficient for you, for my power is made perfect in weakness." Therefore I will boast all the more gladly in my weaknesses so that Christ's power may rest on me.

I, myself, have been laid low by chronic fatigue. In the last two years of graduate school, I was working fifty-to-sixty hours per week on finishing my studies, writing my dissertation, and treating patients at three different locations in San Diego County. On top of that, I was planning my wedding with no family in the area to help me. I was doing and expecting wonderful things, but I was stressed and exhausted. As I got more tired, I tried physical regimens: more jogging or less jogging, more sleep, different nutrition, more caffeine. None of it helped, in fact my fatigue was worsening. I went to medical doctors who tested me for anemia, mononucleosis, and even cancer! None of their tests revealed any problems in my system. But I was in terrible shape. I was so exhausted that my body would involuntarily jerk, I would feel my eyes grow weary and heavy, and worst of all I had a "brain fog" that would overcome my brain so I could not find words or basic information I knew I should know! My symptoms were embarrassing when they happened while I was with my patients, and I tried desperately to hide it from others. I cried out to the Lord over and over to please remove this from me! I cried, "God, can't you see I'm doing *Your* work? Please remove the fatigue so I can do it better!"

Finally, during one of those pleading sessions, the Lord interrupted me, as He sometimes does. He said, "Launi!" and then, in what felt like an exasperated tone, "Don't you understand that *I'm* the one who put this on you? I'm trying to stop you. You are doing too much! I am God, not you! Please slow down, rest, and remember that I am God!" Whoah, that was the opposite of what I expected! But, of course, He was right. I slowed down (a bit), got married to my wonderful husband, and in 1998 we moved to the Seattle area to start our married and career lives. I slowly started up my new private practice and was able to really consider how I wanted to schedule my work time, what kind of patients I wanted to work with and those who would be too draining. I found a naturopathic "cocktail" of four supplements that helped me. After becoming more assertive and balanced in my career choices, the fatigue slowly faded. All in all, my illness lasted about seven years. Thank you, God, for giving me the thorn in my flesh in order to get me to pay attention and know that you are God, not I!

Use of Medications

Medications are proven to be very effective for a wide variety of psychological symptoms. I believe that God has given our medical community the intelligence and means to discover medications that can effectively help His people and reduce their needless suffering. Many of my Christian patients report that they are more effective in their Christian walk (more likely to go to church, read and comprehend their Bible, serve in ministry, etc.) when they are on the proper medications to manage their symptoms. Medications are a tool in the toolbox, an option that all individuals can consider as they make their health care choices. I have come to believe that nobody *wants* to take medication but that they may feel compelled to take it. It often comes down to choosing between the "lesser of two evils"—the hassle and side effects of the medication which helps mood and mind versus no side effects but enduring negative symptoms.

Probably the two most prescribed psychotropic medications for HSPs are antidepressants and short-acting antianxiety medications. The former often works on increasing the effects of serotonin or other neurotransmitters in the brain. Some examples are Prozac, Zoloft, Celexa, and Effexor. These usually take about a week to take effect, and you take a dose once a day. I call these meds the "no brainers" of psychological medications to treat depression and anxiety. They have few side effects and are usually well tolerated. The most problematic potential side effect is a lower sex drive. Some examples of the antianxiety medications include Ativan, Xanax, and Klonopin. These you can take as needed and they work almost instantly to remove a significant amount of the anxiety. They are known to be addicting if the patient overuses them. The HSP is not likely to overuse them, but they will notice a sleepy or dopey effect that they may not like. Likewise, there are naturopathic remedies for depression (such as St. John's wort and Sam-e) and anxiety (such as kava or valerian root), but again, I would advise the HSP to be careful to notice how these affect them and only work with a professional naturopath if they seek these remedies.

What I have noticed among my HSP patients is that they are extremely sensitive to both the intended effects of prescribed medication and the side effects. When doctors prescribe medications, they often start a person on the lowest dose of the typically effective dosage range. Even at this level, HSP patients often feel a "weird" or "flat" effect or notice some other strong effect. This often causes them anxiety, and they either stop taking the medication (and are less likely to take any medications in the future) or talk with their doctor about it and get the dose reduced or the medication changed. I have heard more than one story of the doctor looking at them quizzically and stating something like, "Well, you shouldn't be feeling *that* on *this* dose!" The patient often wonders if the doctor thinks they have "psyched" themselves into their medication reaction or if they will now be labelled as "noncooperative" or "difficult." What I recommend is that HSP patients tell the doctor that they have a highly sensitive system and that they'd like to start at a quarter or half of the typical starting dose. This usually leads the HSP to have a much more helpful experience with the medication. For an HSP taking medication, "A little goes a long way." Of course many people, HSP or non-HSP, decide not to use medications. This is entirely a fair choice to make, and is often where psychologists such as myself can step in and recommend more cognitive, behavioral, and/or spiritual methods of change.

Chapter Five
God, Do I Fit In Here?
Being an HSP in the Social World

God created all people to be innately social, to want to connect with others in meaningful and intimate ways. This is true of HSPs as much as anyone else. However, interpersonal interactions give rise to many complex social stimuli, which can be overwhelming for an HSP. I often describe HSPs as human tuning forks—they vibrate at the same pitch that a nearby human or humans are vibrating at. They can't help it and they can't stop it. So if a person nearby is very upset, the HSP will experience that same feeling of being upset at a lower level. This is helpful for empathic reasons but can be very draining and even intimidating for an HSP.

Sometimes this sensitivity extends to secret spiritual warfare in those close to the HSP. At least three times, female patients of mine have described having dreams where they see an image of their husband being bound by snakes; surrounded by dark, evil wraith-like spirits; or mesmerized by some evil entity. These women were of varying degrees of self-identified spirituality. All of them were Christian but not necessarily of "deep" faith or spiritual practices. In each case, only *after* time had passed from the point where the women saw the visions was it revealed that their husband was engaged in secret sexual sins, such as engaging in sex with prostitutes, watching pornography, or having affairs during the times of the women's visions. These women never told anyone about the images they saw because they weren't sure why they had seen them and they worried others would think they were being too dramatic or making it up. I told them that I believed they were sensitive to their husbands' spiritual states due to their own heightened awareness and because God made them "one flesh" with their husband upon marriage.

By adulthood, HSPs have typically learned some strategies to adapt the reactions they have to many different kinds of people. Since childhood, they have had family members, teachers, and peers they have needed to adjust to. Often they have learned what styles of people they do not do well with; ones who drain them. They have learned to keep such people as superficial acquaintances at best, seeking out others (often other HSPs) as true friends. However, there are two types of social environments where the HSP typically has little control over the other types of people around them: work and church.

Work Challenges

Unless you are self-employed or are lucky enough to be the one who makes all the hiring decisions, you have little choice over whom you work with. And these are people with whom you may be spending most of your waking hours! An HSP can use his or her sensitivities to notice what makes the other employees tick. Sort of like poker players who can gauge how they should bet based upon the other players "tells." If you read your coworkers' tells well, you will tend to know when to put yourself out there and when to hold back, and in the long run you will come out ahead. I have noticed for myself and other HSPs that it is important to be aware of one's own motives for studying others' behaviors. You may be tempted to become manipulative based on this ability. Most HSPs, however, are highly conscientious and aware of how their behaviors impact others. The last thing they would want to do is to harm someone or manipulate them. I talk with my patients about developing "communication strategies" for interacting with different personality types.

My patient Grant works in a male-dominated workplace where the guys like to give one another a hard time. Grant was emotionally abused as a child and is therefore doubly sensitive to issues of harassment, bullying, intimidation, and cruelty. He can sense when a person is victimizing others in the name of humor. He has learned to dole it right back to the nonsensitives: He knows they can take it, unlike the HSPs. However, he took his strategy to a higher level. His job is unionized and he took steps to become a union steward so that he could tolerate this difficult workplace, giving him a voice and some degree of power. From what he humbly described to me, he is one of the most sought-out union reps in the company! In this position, Grant can do something productive and helpful with the special information he has from being HSP and can also aid victims and those in less power when he needs to, much as he needed assistance when he was younger.

Another coping strategy is to identify who the other HSPs in your workplace are and perhaps talk with them about what each of them is sensitive to or aware of. You can form a sort of fellowship to help one another. If they are other Christians, you can commit to pray for your workplace together, which will have a positive impact on your workplace (but please be careful to avoid any gossip!). You can pray for any coworker, especially those who are problematic. For me, it has always seemed logical to pray for my "enemies" (See Matthew 5:44). If a person is being challenging to you, it is likely a result of something being seriously amiss in his or her physical, relational, or spiritual life. If you make the choice to genuinely pray for the Lord to help, bless, and or heal the person, he or she will be a happier, more secure person, which will make *your* life better, too!

We have been looking at the emotional strains that can occur for the HSP in the workplace, but there can be physical-sensory-overload situations as well. Many of my HSP patients find open cubicle-type work spaces to be difficult due to the noise and other sensory stimuli (can you say, "Old Spice cologne"?). Some even find the glare from the computer screen to be too much. Many of my patients are hesitant to speak up about their work place challenges because they don't want to appear to be a whiner or weak to their boss or colleagues. They have probably already been told that message in some way by the other 80 percent of the population for most of their lives, and they do not want to hear it again. But it is important to remember that any employer would rather keep a trained, experienced employee over a new hire, especially if that employee is performing at least averagely. If you explain to your employer that you could work even more effectively with some reasonable accommodations, he or she will typically be willing to assist!

Some accommodations my patients have found helpful include: being allowed to wear noise-cancelling headphones in the workplace; having their cubicle in a corner or more secluded, quiet area; having a dimmer computer screen; being allowed to record meetings and conversations in order to process them more deeply later in a less-stimulating atmosphere; and so forth. Perhaps the most important accommodation to seek is a quiet place to retreat to during the workday. Many people have one that they go to during their lunch breaks or when they are taking a walk outside the building. Some find an unused area in the building that they can "hide" out in for even ten minutes.

My patient, Stuart, included on his schedule an extended lunch break. He would close the door to his office, listen to music on his headphones, and savor his homemade lunch. Once his lunch was finished, he would either read his Bible, a favorite book (typically one that fed his spiritual needs), or take a nap. Not all of Stuart's coworkers understood his need for this buffer time, and being an HSP, he could feel their confusion and sometimes their consternation. However, many of his office mates learned to allow him this "down time," knowing he would be ready to finish off his day with his usual diligence and excellent work when he emerged. Stuart now accepts that he is an HSP, he cannot change that, and he has the right and need to set limits to accommodate his HSP needs. He learned he needed to speak up for his lunch break the hard way: At his previous job he had become so burnt out that he would pull to the side of the road and cry in his car at the thought of going back to work again. He had to leave that job, but we discussed how he could enter the new job with new assertive requests. After our planning and role-play rehearsals, Stuart was able to create a better work environment for himself in the new job.

Some easy ways to soften and brighten up your work space are the adding of live plants, photos of those you love, and anything that will prompt you to laugh when you see it (it's very hard to be scared or angry when you are laughing!). One of my patients carried a porcelain frog with her to any workplace she worked in. She had a deal with God that whenever her eyes would light upon the frog, she would pray.

Another consideration regarding work, if financially plausible, is to work part time or on call. The benefit of working on call is that you can ultimately choose to go into work based upon how your nervous system has been feeling. However, a downside is that your body does not have the assurance of a regular schedule.

When you feel at the end of your rope at work, try remembering this verse: "Whatever you do, work at it with all your heart, as working for the Lord, not for human masters" (Colossians 3:23–24). Ultimately your workplace boss is not your true boss. You desire to please your heavenly Father first and foremost. Your Heavenly Boss knows all your strengths and weaknesses—He made you! He will give you the strength and perseverance to continue when you are feeling overwhelmed, and He will also give you a way out if you need it, as He did for my patient I just described who finally found himself crying on the way to work.

Church Challenges

It can be so difficult to find a great fit when choosing a church: a place where you can feel free to love the Lord and your Christian family. For HSPs, this can be particularly challenging because they are attuned to so many equally important aspects: the presence of the Spirit in the church, the sound and quality of the worship music, the "culture" or vibe of the church (casual or formal, for instance), and a myriad of other aspects. My husband and I had moved to a new neighborhood and were church shopping when our first two children were a preschooler and a toddler. I rejected several churches simply based upon the "energy" I felt in the Sunday-school rooms. When church shopping, you will likely want your spouse to be aware of your experience as an HSP and what you are picking up with your "spidey senses," (ala Spiderman sensing negative intents nearby). This will help your spouse to be more understanding and patient with what may seem to be your "picky" process. Remind your spouse that in the long run it is important for you to find the right church fit, or you won't be happy there (which means your spouse won't be happy, either!).

For many years, my husband and I attended a large church of over three thousand members. We greatly enjoyed the teaching from the pulpit there and were able to make some good friends from a small home group that we attended. However, every Christmas and Easter was a spectacle. Parking became impossible, and the church even had to use shuttle buses! Finding a seat, let alone at the service you originally planned to attend, was equally frustrating. I was totally overwhelmed by the experience and refused to attend any more of the Christmas and Easter sermons at that church. These were two holidays that mean so much to me on a spiritual level and I sorely missed the experience of communal worship. It seems to me that the last thing you want is for your church's culture itself to distract you from your communion with the Lord. In the meantime, we moved to a more rural neighborhood. We did a church search in our new neighborhood and attended five different churches. We finally found a small, friendly country-style church of about three hundred members, and we truly feel like we have found our church family! So, please don't give up on looking for a church that is a good fit. The Lord desires for us to be in fellowship in His name (Hebrews 10:24–25). Even if it is not a perfect fit, you will hopefully feel comfortable enough to use your sensitivities to promote positive change in the church, which will also be very gratifying to you.

Once you find a church that seems to be a good fit, there will still be challenges to overcome with your interpersonal relationships there. You can choose your church, but you cannot choose who you will be sharing it with! One of the difficulties of attending a church is that there will be requests for volunteers to serve the church or wider community. The desire to serve is typically strong for HSPs, but it is tempered by fears of being burnt by others who may seem critical of how they are doing things. You see, typically HSPs are not inclined toward leadership roles. Although HSPs are very conscientious and responsible in general, the natural attention and criticism that come with leadership can feel overwhelming and intimidating for them. Therefore leadership positions tend to be held by non-HSPs who, in an effort to get things accomplished, may come across as too harsh for an HSP.

One of my HSP patients truly enjoyed serving in a children's ministry and found that her own faith was deepening because of it. However, she found it almost unbearable to be questioned or to have assistants who wanted to do things in a different way than she did. She would wonder, "Are they trying to tell me I'm doing it wrong? Are they frustrated with me?" These are common overanalyzing thoughts for an HSP but they could have ultimately driven her out of that ministry! She was able to stay in her position partly because she would bring these fearful thoughts to our sessions and we would review the evidence. The evidence suggested that she was performing just fine and there were issues she was picking up on that had nothing to do with her. After a couple of years in the same position of serving toddlers, she developed a sense of mastery. She would never be questioned by the little tikes she so easily won over, and when an assistant would try to do things differently from her she would just decide in her mind that she and the assistant could divide up the work tasks so they could do it their own ways. She no longer needed to take anything personally in the environment, and she began to enjoy the ministry even more!

Another way that volunteering can be difficult for HSPs is simply that it can lead to "burnout" when they have done too much. Usually, in any given church, only a few of the congregants do most of the work. Let's face it, there are many who appear to be flaky and not doing their part. This can lead to a feeling of frustration for the already-tired volunteer HSP. The HSP will in turn think he or she has been judgmental, leading to feelings of guilt. After all, we are called to love one another, not berate others in our minds, right? Here again is a perfect time to shift our perspective from our puny, momentary experience and focus on the power of God to intervene. Lift up these circumstances and give them over to the Lord! Remember the serenity prayer: "Lord, grant me the serenity to accept the things I cannot change, the courage to change the things I can, and the wisdom to know the difference." We do not know the inner reasons why our fellow churchgoers appear to be sitting on the sidelines. For all we know, they could be burnt-out HSPs! Our Heavenly Father knows it all too clearly, and it is our privilege to lift up our church body in prayer as well as our own responses to it.

In the meantime, you can "let your 'yes' be yes and your 'no' no" (James 5:12) and set healthy expectations for your part to play in the church. Even our good and perfect Lord, Jesus, would remove himself from the fray in order to go to a solitary place to pray (for example, see Matthew 14:23). He has felt all the feelings that we have felt in his humanness. He knew He needed a balance between the press of work and the renewal of rest. Take a lesson from Him, and learn to balance your commitments so that you won't suffer burnout and bench yourself on the sidelines!

HSP and Spiritual Gifts

I did some preliminary research to determine if there are any correlations between the spiritual gifts (for example, see 1 Corinthians 12) and being an HSP. I gave a survey packet to my patients who wanted to take part and to women at our church women's retreat as well as to men and women at our denomination's family camp. The total number of people who participated is forty-eight. The packet included the HSP self-test, a survey about spiritual gifts designed by Bruce Bugbee,[12] and some open-ended questions regarding serving in the church, psychological diagnoses or symptoms, and what aspects of church most affected them.

In terms of spiritual gifts, in my research the only three spiritual gifts that have a significant positive correlation with being an HSP are craftsmanship ($p = .031$), discernment ($p = .034$), and encouragement ($p = .050$). Two spiritual gifts are significantly *negatively* correlated with being an HSP: leadership ($p = .037$) and teaching (approaching significance at $p = .060$). Let's unpack these findings.

From my results, it appears that being highly sensitive is most associated with the gift of craftsmanship. Craftsmanship, in Bugbee's survey, is described as "the divine enablement to creatively design and/or construct items to be used for ministry."[13]

---

[12]. Bugbee, Bruce. *Discover Your Spiritual Gifts the Network Way*. Grand Rapids, MI: Zondervan, 2005.

[13] Bugbee, Bruce. Discover Your Spiritual Gifts the Network Way. Pg. 59

This was not what I expected to be the top spiritual gift correlated with being an HSP! My subject population is 70 percent female, and in my church experiences it seems like women do not often serve in positions of physical maitenance. I believe this finding about craftsmanship must therefore be due to the aspect, common in HSPs, of being able to see a tangible need and creatively design the solution. HSPs seem to truly have some unique abilities to observe overt and subtle needs in the environment and to want to enhance the environment for their own and others' benefits.

The next-highest correlation is between being an HSP and discernment. This was exactly what I had expected would be highly correlated with being an HSP. Bugbee describes discernment as "the divine enablement to distinguish between truth and error. It is the ability to discern the spirits, differentiating between good and evil, right and wrong."[14] I intuitively suspected that being sensitive to sensory input would include being sensitive to spiritual "input." Remember how I compared being HSP to being a human tuning fork? I believe HSPs are more susceptible to picking up the "vibrations" of good and evil, and God uses this in the gift of discernment. In this way, HSPs can use their gift of discernment to powerfully pray for God's goodness to prevail and to rebuke evil as they see these forces at work around them. In fact, the second-most-chosen area of service by my subject pool was "praying for others," which they found extremely gratifying.

The third-most-correlated spiritual gift is encouragement. Bugbee describes encouragement as "the divine enablement to present truth so as to strengthen, comfort, or urge to action those who are discouraged or wavering in their faith."[15] Again, this one seemed to be a natural fit. HSPs tend to pick up on the inner and outer needs of others and find peace in reducing their sufferings as well as joy at seeing them become happier and closer to the Lord.

[14] Bugbee, Bruce. Discover Your Spiritual Gifts the Network Way. Pg. 59

[15] Bugbee, Bruce. Discover Your Spiritual Gifts the Network Way. Pg. 59

HSPs are known for being conscientious. They can barely stand to see a need and not do something about it in their own "behind-the-scenes" kind of way. Almost all of my HSP research participants described intense gratification at helping others, particularly in helping others to become closer to the Lord. The only negative aspects of this that they reported were becoming fatigued and not being able to do more, or being discouraged that there weren't more people assisting in their service efforts.

It is not surprising to me that leadership and teaching are negatively associated with being an HSP. HSPs tend to shy away from the limelight where they are more prone to scrutiny and criticism. The pressures in these areas take a great toll on the HSP who would rather assist those who are in leadership than be the leader him or herself.

Now let's review the primary areas where HSPs are likely to serve the church. Firstly, it is notable that only three HSPs in my study stated that they were not actively serving the church. Two of the three indicated that they used to serve others but are not doing so at this time. I tend to think that these individuals fall into my "burnt" or "burned-out" categories. However, the other HSPs overwhelmingly stated that they serve their church.

By far the most common way they serve is with children and youth. Again, this does not surprise me. Children and youth tend to be loving, accepting, and open to direction more often than adults. Adults are more empowered and inclined to be critical, judgmental, or close minded. I asked all my participants to tell me what they enjoyed about serving the church, and also what they did *not* like about serving in their specific way. Some of the positive comments from the participants who serve children are that they particularly enjoy "[kids'] honesty and acceptance," "expressing, sharing God's love," "knowing I made a difference," and "helping someone learn and grow," and a couple of others state, "Kids are fun to be around" and "Encouraging children is rewarding." Some of the negative comments about serving children include that participants find it difficult "preparing the lesson and difficult children" and that it is "discouraging to see children who have not been given home discipline, so they find it hard to cooperate in a group setting." Some other less-enthusiastic comments are, "Sometimes the kids are loud and chaotic," "Sometimes I don't know what to do with a child or feel like a failure. It can be exhausting," "I do not like being the only or one of a few to help the youth of our community," and "[There is] not enough direction or vision for class yet," "Sometimes the environment can be overwhelming. I do not like working with overjudgmental people or overbearing [people]." Others suggest that they don't enjoy "the risk of rejection or lack of progress" and "being obligated to be 'on' and look happy when sometimes I don't feel it (mostly with adults, not the kids)."[16]

The second-most-common area of service for my HSP participants is "praying for others." This fits very easily with the "tuning fork" gift of discernment noted earlier. Some of the comments HSPs offered about the positive aspects of praying for others are that they enjoy "helping others accept Christ...having people tell me they are changing because of Jesus," "encouraging others, helping them grow in Christ," "praying when others are silent or can't verbalize problems," "sharing a positive daily attitude and praise to God for His provisions," "praying because I can be quiet and I don't have to have all the answers," and "the feeling that even if I can't change things for [others], I've given them hope by helping them tap into the One who can," and one stated, "sending cards reminds me to pray specifically for and about that individual." Some of the negative aspects of serving in prayer they shared are, "I *hope* He will help those I pray for. I'm no longer *certain* He will," "Usually I'm praying from a list provided by my church, so I don't get to be with the person I'm praying for, and I

---

[16]All quotes in the preceding and following paragraphs are of handwritten comments by particpants in my research survey, conducted in 2011.

seldom find out the outcome or see God's answer to my prayers," and "[I dislike] having to rebuke others."

The third-most-common area of service for my HSP participants is hospitality. This area fits nicely with the ability HSPs have to sense what would make others feel more comfortable, and perhaps overlaps with the spiritual gift of craftsmanship. Some of the positive statements HSPs made about hospitality are that they enjoy "saying good morning with a smile on my face," "helping new people get connected," "making others feel welcome," "helping others that can't help themselves because it brings joy and fulfillment to my heart and soul. It makes me feel wonderful knowing I might have made a change in someone's life and that I touched them in some way that made them happy," and "hosting [in the form of] having people visit." Respondents also shared some negative comments about serving in the form of hospitality, saying that they don't appreciate "being available and being expected to do it" and "always trying to get people to help," and "when I prepare for people to come over and they don't show up and don't call to tell you that they aren't coming." That last one was finished off with a sad face drawn in, and who can blame her! My heart breaks for her just reading her words!

Finally, the following areas of service for my HSP survey participants ranked fourth, fifth, sixth and seventh: teaching, music, administration, and "all of the above." I found it interesting that when asked what aspects of church most affect them, the HSPs almost unanimously chose "music"; however, not many actually serve in this area. One of the HSPs who serves in music wrote this: "Playing guitar on the worship team allows me to use gifts and talents that He gave me to further His kingdom, (but) playing on the worship team exposes my inabilities and mistakes." I believe that although music deeply moves HSPs more than the average person, they are inhibited from performing in that arena due to discomfort with being "on stage" and potentially judged.

Interestingly, research is showing that HSPs tend to perform better on tasks than non-HSPs; however, they also experience more stress while doing the tasks.[17] I imagine that the guitar player just quoted performs just fine at playing worship music but is stressed at his own expectations and perceptions and worries that others will have the same expectations and perceptions of him as he has of himself. If he were my patient, I would encourage him with the probability that eighty percent of the congregation does not notice or care about subtleties as much as he does. The other 20 percent may notice but are generally empathic for him if he makes a mistake. They may even be praying for him to do his best and will offer him words of encouragement when he is done!

Like a Tree...

Ultimately, our purpose and joy in life is found in the Lord, not His people. I first found out I was an HSP a few years ago. I was coming up on my forty-second birthday and was absolutely dreading it. I decided I did not want to dread my birthday for the rest of my life, so I returned to counseling to talk about what was bothering me about my birthday. I had not worked with this therapist before, and I explained that I was a Christian and that I'd had a horrific fortieth birthday. I had wanted one of those full-blown fortieth-birthday gala events. I figured that it was the last big birthday I'd have unless I make it to a hundred, and I looked forward to partying with my friends and family. I had thrown a successful surprise fortieth party for my husband the year before, and now he wanted to surprise me as well. The party was at a video arcade in downtown Seattle. The one major problem with my birthday is it has a very unfortunate date: December 28. Although he invited all of my friends and family

---

17. Friederike Gerstenberg, "Sensory-Processing Sensitivity Predicts Performance on a Visual Search Task Followed by an Increase in Perceived Stress," *Personality and Individual Differences* 53 (2010), 496–500.

(about a hundred people), in the end nobody came except our pastor and his family.

In desperation, my husband asked my mother who lived with us to come at the last minute, and she agreed (my mother loves me, but being HSP herself she had originally declined since the noise and atmosphere would be too much for her). She called my stepfather to leave work early so that he could attend, too. My husband had already bought tickets for other friends and family who had said they would come but then cancelled at the last minute. So he went next door to a family of eleven to ask if they would come and they did. It was a horrible experience to sit through the event knowing that only five people were truly there for me of their own accord and that so many had decided it was not worth the effort. I also had a very difficult time on my forty-first birthday as so many bad memories came back. Now I was approaching my forty-second birthday and I wanted to conquer the feelings that this event had created in me. My therapist kindly explained to me about being an HSP. Once I accepted this description of myself, she directed my attention to a passage of scripture in Jeremiah 17:5–8 that states:

> Cursed is the one who trusts in man,
> Who depends on flesh for his strength
> And whose heart turns away from the Lord.
> He will be like a bush in the wastelands;
> He will not see prosperity when it comes.
> He will dwell in the parched places of the desert,
> In a salt land where no one lives.
> But blessed is the man who trusts in the Lord,
> Whose confidence is in Him.
> He will be like a tree planted by the water
> That sends out its roots by the stream.
> It does not fear when heat comes;
> Its leaves are always green.

It has no worries in a year of drought
And never fails to bear fruit.

My therapist explained that this scripture has helped her to cope with her own HSP qualities by allowing her to learn to not place too many hopes and expectations in other humans but rather to focus on the presence and life support of the Lord. This scripture has blessed me too. I can see how as an HSP it is easy to feel hurt and misunderstood by others. It's easy to feel hurt and confused when others do not care for you in the same way that you care for them. However, with the Lord I am always perfectly understood, for He created me. He will always care for me, no matter what other people do or fail to do. I choose to see myself as a tree planted by water whose roots reach down to the water that is His life. This rootedness makes me fruitful and steadfast, though the winds of the worldly challenges blow the rest of me around. My sustenance will be the Lord and it will never cease to nurture me, even though other humans may let me down and disappoint me by not showing up for an important birthday! You may be wondering what advice my therapist gave me for handling future birthdays. She suggested that I plan each birthday just as *I* wanted it to be and that I only involve my husband or maybe just a couple of close friends. That way, it will always be what I want and a guaranteed success. I really enjoyed my forty-second birthday at a bed and breakfast getaway with my husband, and I look forward to my future birthdays now. My husband feels so badly about my fortieth that I think I can get away with planning special birthdays for the rest of my life! So you see this cloud had two silver linings: I learned about being HSP (which has allowed me to help other HSPs), and I now get some great birthdays just the way I like them!

Chapter Six

God, You Made Me Strong!
Unique Strengths of the HSP

HSPs are uniquely suited to perceive where something is amiss and to step in with prayer, advice, or a helping hand. Do you remember Joe? He became aware that two women in his general work vicinity had recently had babies and were back at work yet needed to use the breast pump during the day to keep up their milk supply. He found a storage room that was little used and spruced it up with comfy chairs, end tables, magazines, and posters. He placed a sign on the door that stated, "Nursing moms only." He asked the women if this was helpful to them and they were very appreciative of his thoughtfulness. I think Joe felt even better about being able to serve them than they did about having a relaxing, private place to pump.

Hospitality

This leads to another way that being an HSP can be a blessing to others: hospitality. An HSP can tell when others are feeling comfortable or not. They can sense what would make a room feel welcoming and warm. They would make excellent hosts for a small group meeting or facilitating other small groups, such as a Celebrate Recovery group. Celebrate Recovery (see http://www.celebraterecovery.com) is a way for churches to reach out to the community and offer free, layperson-led support groups for a variety of issues. The original focus was on addiction-type issues, but it can be expanded to cover virtually any issue people are seeking support for (such as divorce recovery, grief, etc.). Typically, an HSP is highly empathic, which is likely why I found in my research that this type of person is also gifted with encouragement. HSPs may want to consider becoming trained as a Steven's minister (lay counselor for a church) or to assist with congregational care outreach. Several of the participants in my study stated that they enjoyed writing cards to church members.

Stepping up into hospitality can bring with it an opening for frustration and hurt feelings. Perhaps those you are caring for do not appreciate it, or simply don't show up (is it only the HSPs who actually RSVP anymore?). Perhaps you will receive negative feedback on how you are leading the group. I myself have felt these concerns and fears as I stepped up to host a church home group or lead small groups. One thing I found helpful for myself is to purposefully solicit feedback. I have found that when I proactively seek praises or criticisms people seem more willing to give me honest feedback. Most of the time the feedback is positive and encouraging. Like most HSPs, I really thrive on the "Atta girl!" comments and need to hear them to feel encouraged to go on. When I do receive constructive criticism, I find it very helpful in making my efforts more effective, which is also encouraging to me. But I can only count on one hand the times I asked for feedback and it ended up being worse than I had feared. Remember the story of the nonsensitive public speaker who brought me to heaving sobs? I recently, with great trepidation, reviewed a handwritten sheet of paper from that session. It was intended to provide me written feedback so that I would remember how I performed and the tips given to me after the fact. I do not know if it was written by the teacher or the vetted public speaker member, but I was surprised at some of the positive wording. At the top of the page were written two scripture messages for me:

Listen, my son, accept what I say,

And the years of your life will be many.
I instruct you in the way of wisdom
And lead you along straight paths.
When you walk, your steps will not be hampered;
When you run, you will not stumble.
Hold on to instruction, do not let it go.
Guard it well, for it is your life.
(Proverbs 4:10–13)

Now Daniel so distinguished himself among
The administrators and the satraps by his
Exceptional qualities that the king planned to
Set him over the whole kingdom.
(Daniel 6:3)

After that scripture the author wrote, "Excellent character in you. God has called you to great things. You have a gift." Hmmmm...wow...I had been so wounded by the harsh, insensitive way I had received the negative (and accurate) feedback about my speaking skills that I could not even bear to look at this paper until this recent date, almost three years later. I regret that I did not have the courage to look at it and receive the good messages sooner. The Lord ultimately redeemed His mission for me, despite my burnt spirit, by encouraging me to write this book. I pray for you that you will have more courage than I have, in being ready to hear, see, and receive plenty of positive, life-giving messages in life and also in being able to take the negative feedback as messages to make you even stronger (perhaps along the way you will find more morels and avoid all the poisonous red mushrooms!). Remember always, though, that like a tree planted by water, your worth and Life come from the Father, Jesus, and the Holy Spirit, not from any human.

Proactive Decision Making

HSPs are more aware of subtle nuances, which can guide more effective decisions. They may be able to notice patterns in the environment, thereby making their predictions more accurate. However, HSPs are also often overwhelmed by being in positions of leadership, so they will tend to prefer to guide from the background.

Do you recall Elizabeth, who memorized Proverbs 3 and who tended to worry on behalf of others? She was able to observe a subtle different pattern in her husband that saved his life! Her husband's complaints were mild and vague, such as fatigue, but she could tell that "something was wrong." She nagged him to make an appointment to see his doctor (does that sound familiar to anyone?), but when he went, the doctor could find nothing wrong with him and sent him home with the suggestion that he rest. She felt chagrined, and a tad embarrassed, that the doctor found nothing wrong. Yet she *knew* she was sensing something that did not add up in her husband's mannerisms and complaints of being tired. Elizabeth persisted and insisted that her husband go back to the doctors for a second opinion, and she went along with him to his doctor's visit to assist in the process. This time, after deeper testing, the doctors diagnosed that he had leukemia and started treatment immediately. Although she had felt that she was being a bit of a nag, and was sensitive to the sting of dismissiveness, she is ultimately proud of herself (and her husband is eternally grateful) for listening to her intuition.

As I said before, I refer to this sixth sense of intuition as being like my "spidey senses." I can tell my husband that "my spidey senses are tingling," and he becomes curious as to what I am cluing into. Sometimes those senses can alert me to avoid contact or relationships with people who just don't altogether feel safe to me. As a psychologist, I know too well that there are individuals in our society who seek to use others, even children, for their own evil intent. As a mom, I am particularly concerned that none of my children are ever abused or used.

Our family loves to vacation at our church denomination's family camp at the base of beautiful Mount Rainier. It is very peaceful and fun, nestled in among the evergreens. The children's favorite places to play are the creek and the woods near the main grassy field. It would be possible for an abuser to sequester them alone. I quickly tuned into the unfamiliar teenagers and adults around me and watched how they interacted with the children. All of them felt very safe and secure, except I was not sure about one adult man. He seemed to always be watching my four-year-old daughter as she flitted about the cafeteria. He would make a point to come over to her and kneel down at eye level to talk with her with a big smile on his face. He asked us many questions about her—he seemed very intrigued with her. My daughter is a blond, blue-eyed, sweet, and friendly girl, so I've always known (and feared) that she would attract the attention of others. Without telling my husband, I decided to keep my own very watchful eye on this man and really try to get his "angle." In the meantime, I made sure I always knew where my daughter was and where he was. I will confess that I tended to think that my negative assumptions about his intentions were correct. When it comes to protecting my child, I guess I err on the side of "Guilty until proven innocent."

Thankfully, this story is an example of how an HSP like me can be observant but overly anxious (or "paranoid" as I sometimes call myself). Over the next few days, I saw no evidence to support my fears. Just the opposite, I saw evidence that this man truly cared for young children. He delighted in their innocence and joie de vivre. Afterward, I felt some pangs of guilt at my inner false accusations of character, but I also took some reassurance in my ability to be proactive in the case of real or potential danger to myself or others. As a footnote, I tend to think that man was not an HSP. HSP men are usually very aware that parents of small children, even the children themselves, might feel "creepy" about excessive attention being paid to their kids and would tend to be more subdued in their interactions with children. Certainly they would pick up on any tensions the parents were feeling and back off as needed.

Weakness *Is* a Strength

So is being a highly sensitive person a burden or a blessing? A mixture of God-given strengths or a hodgepodge of frustrating weaknesses? I hope that I have conveyed to HSPs reading this book that there are many positives about being an HSP and many ways God can uniquely use your traits. At the same time, I hope I have conveyed that it is understandable if you sometimes feel overwhelmed, anxious, or depressed about being an HSP. At times, being an HSP certainly can feel more like a weakness than a strength, and frankly sometimes it is. However, in our weakness, or thorn in our side, God's strength is made clearer to us and those around us, because it is only by His grace that we can get through this challenging world.

I am so grateful that God does not just tell us to have faith in His strength, pat us on the head, and then send us out the door into the big, wide world. With our sensitivities, we would feel extremely vulnerable and exposed if He worked this way. He has instead created a very special suit of armor for us to wear into the world.

As instructed in Ephesians 6:13–18:

> Put on the full armor of God...to stand. Stand firm then, with the belt of truth buckled around your waist, with the breastplate of righteousness in place, and with your feet fitted with the readiness that comes from the gospel of peace. In addition to all this, take up the shield of faith, with which you can extinguish all the flaming arrows of the evil one. Take the helmet of salvation and the sword of the Spirit, which is the word of God. And pray in the Spirit on all

occasions with all kinds of prayers and requests. With this in mind be alert...

That last line, "pray in the Spirit on all occasions with all kinds of prayers and requests," I believe, points to perhaps the greatest strength of the Christian HSP. As you have seen from my examples in this book, HSPs have a unique awareness that guides their prayers in powerful ways. The enemy would like to distract them from praying down God's power to help with the dangers of this world and instead focus their energies on merely surviving the dangers. Take courage and harness your sensitivities for His purposes.

God's word and promises are truly more than sufficient to help us manage this world and help it become a better place when we use our HSP strengths to give to those around us. I particularly like the fact that the Word calls us to "stand" and be "alert." As HSPs, we have no problem with being alert. You could say we were made to be alert! But with God's armor, we can also stand firm instead of running from what our alertness tells us to do. We can be effectively used as His servant for His kingdom come here on Earth. Can there be any greater privilege than that?

Bibliography

Aron, Elaine N. "Author's Note, 2012." Last modified September 6, 2012, http://hsperson.com.

———. *The Highly Sensitive Person*. New York: Carol Publishing Group, 1996.

———. *Psychotherapy and the Highly Sensitive Person*. New York: Taylor and Francis Group, 2010.

———. "Sensory-Processing Sensitivity and Its Relation to Introversion and Emotionality." *Journal of Personality and Social Psychology* 73, no. 2 (1997): 345-368.

Bartz, Andrea. "Sense and Sensitivity." *Psychology Today* 72, last modified July 22, 2014, https://www.psychologytoday.com/articles/201107/sense-and-sensitivity.

Bugbee, Bruce. *Discover Your Spiritual Gifts the Network Way*. Grand Rapids, MI: Zondervan, 2005.

Gerstenberg, Friederike, "Sensory-Processing Sensitivity Predicts Performance on a Visual Search Task Followed by an Increase in Perceived Stress." *Personality and Individual Differences* 53 (2010): 496–500.

Heller, Sharon. *Too Loud Too Bright Too Fast Too Tight*. New York: Harper Collins, 2002.

Holmes TH, Rahe RH (1967). "The Social Readjustment Rating Scale". *Journal of Psychosomatic Research* 11 (2): 213–218.

Jawer, Michael A. and Marc S. Micozzi. *The Spiritual Anatomy of Emotion*. Rochester, VT: Park Street Press, 2009.

Smolewska, Kathy A., Scott B. McCabe, and Erik Z. Woody. "A Psychometric Evaluation of the Highly Sensitive Person Scale: The Components of Sensory-Processing Sensitivity and Their Relation to the BIS/BAS and 'Big Five.'" *Personality and Individual Differences* 40 (2006).

Appendix A

Are You Highly Sensitive?
A Self-Test

Instructions: Answer each question according to what you feel is accurate about you. Circle "True" if the statement at least moderately describes you. Circle "False" if the statement doesn't really describe you or doesn't describe you at all.

I am easily overwhelmed by strong sensory input.	T	F
I seem to be aware of subtleties in my environment.	T	F
Other people's moods affect me.	T	F
I tend to be very sensitive to pain.	T	F
I find myself needing to withdraw during busy days, into bed or into a darkened room or any place where I can have some privacy and relief from stimulation.	T	F
I am particularly sensitive to the effects of caffeine.	T	F
I am easily overwhelmed by things like bright lights, strong smells, coarse fabrics, or sirens close by.	T	F
I have a rich, complex inner life.	T	F
I am made uncomfortable by loud noises.	T	F
I am deeply moved by the arts or music.	T	F
My nervous system sometimes feels so frazzled that I just have to get away by myself.	T	F
I am conscientious.	T	F
I startle easily.	T	F
I get rattled when I have a lot to do in a short amount of time.	T	F

When people are uncomfortable in a physical environment, I tend to know what needs to be done to make it more comfortable (like changing the lighting or the seating).	(T)	F
I am annoyed when people try to get me to do too many things at once.	T	F
I try hard to avoid making mistakes or forgetting things.	(T)	F
I make it a point to avoid violent movies and TV shows.	T	F
I become unpleasantly aroused when a lot is going on around me.	(T)	F
Being very hungry creates a strong reaction in me, disrupting my concentration or mood.	(T)	F
Changes in my life shake me up.	T	F
I notice and enjoy delicate or fine scents, tastes, sounds, and works of art.	T	F
I find it unpleasant to have a lot going on at once.	T	F
I make it a high priority to arrange my life to avoid upsetting or overwhelming situations.	T	F
When I must complete or be observed while performing a task, I become so nervous or shaky that I do much worse than I would otherwise.	(T)	F
When I was a child, my parents or teachers seemed to see me as sensitive or shy.	(T)	F
SCORE	10/12	

Note: Adapted from Elaine N. Aron, *The Highly Sensitive Person*. New York: Carol Publishing Group, 1996. Minor revisions added to the instructions, the True and False columns, and the Score row.

Scoring the self-test for high sensitivity

If you answered more than fourteen of the questions as true of yourself, you are probably highly sensitive. But frankly, no psychological test is so accurate that an individual should base his or her life on the results. We psychologists try to develop good questions and then decide on the base level for qualifying by using the average response. If fewer questions are true of you, but *extremely* true, that might also justify calling yourself highly sensitive, especially if you are male.

Additional information about highly sensitive persons is available at http://hsperson.com.

Manufactured by Amazon.ca
Bolton, ON